MODERN CHRISTIAN LITERATURE

IS VOLUME

119

OF THE

Twentieth Century Encyclopedia of Catholicism

UNDER SECTION

XI

CATHOLICISM AND LITERATURE

IT IS ALSO THE

62ND

VOLUME IN ORDER OF PUBLICATION

Edited by **HENRI DANIEL-ROPS** *of the Académie Française*

MODERN
CHRISTIAN LITERATURE

By GISBERT KRANZ

Translated from the French by J. R. FOSTER

HAWTHORN BOOKS · PUBLISHERS · *New York*

First Edition, March, 1961

NIHIL OBSTAT

Joannes M. T. Barton, S.T.D., L.S.S.

Censor Deputatus

IMPRIMATUR

E. Morrogh Bernard

Vicarius Generalis

Westmonasterii, die XXVI JANUARII MCMLXI

CONTENTS

INTRODUCTION

The aim of this book is to provide a reasonably detailed description, interpretation and criticism of a number of books; as a result a selection according to fixed criteria had to be made from the host of modern Christian writers. Forty-one authors were left, and this selection may be considered complete of its kind.

Christian literature is here used to mean only books dealing directly with Christian doctrine, history or piety and written in a Christian spirit. This restriction to religious writing involves a certain narrowness of approach which will be regretted by everyone who, like the author himself, regards Cervantes' *Don Quixote*, Shakespeare's plays, Gotthelf's[1] novels and Stifter's[2] stories as all belonging to Christian literature. On the other hand, the net has been cast wide enough to include all European countries and denominations: Germany, France, England, Spain, Italy, Holland, Russia and Denmark are all represented, and by the side of Catholic writers stand Lutheran, Calvinist, Anglican, Puritan and Orthodox ones as well. Indeed in some of the religious writers and thinkers discussed in this book there are strong non-Christian elements; this is particularly the case with Milton and Novalis, although in those of their works considered here the Christian element outweighs

[1] Jeremias Gotthelf was the pseudonym of Albert Bitzius (1797–1854), a Protestant clergyman who wrote novels of Swiss country life with a markedly Christian flavour. Gotthelf's German is strongly coloured with Bernese dialect; this makes translation difficult and has prevented his novels from enjoying the wide reputation which they undoubtedly deserve. See J. R. Foster, "Jeremias Gotthelf," *Dublin Review*, 465 (1954). (*Trans.*)

[2] Adalbert Stifter (1805–68), the greatest prose-writer of nineteenth-century Austria, wrote two novels and a large number of shorter tales. (*Trans.*)

all others. Paracelsus, Böhme, Swedenborg, Blake and other similar Gnostics, in whom the Christian tradition is heavily overlaid by extraneous borrowings, would be out of place in a book of this sort.

By Christian *literature* we mean only works of high literary and artistic rank, works universally regarded as part of world literature, which have made their influence felt beyond the boundaries of their own age, land and denomination, and are looked upon as common property of lasting value. On the other hand, the term is allowed to include didactic prose as well as imaginative literature proper: sermons, history, philosophy, theology and devotional and mystical writings are all included.

By *modern* Christian literature we mean literature written between 1517 and 1917, between the start of the Reformation and the start of the Russian revolution: authors like Claudel, Jammes, Chesterton and Belloc, who published important work before the First World War but only established their reputations after it, have been left outside our survey.

The restriction to works of modern literature which are documents of Christian faith, that is, to books which bear the twin seal of nobility of mind and piety, brings to light some noteworthy facts. The sixteenth century, from the religious point of view a century of collapse, destruction and renewal, can point to only six great Christian writers, while the seventeenth century is represented by eighteen authors: Calderon, Sales, Pascal, Bossuet, Fénelon, Corneille, Racine, Donne, Crashaw, Bunyan, Milton, Bidermann, Spee, Silesius, Gerhardt, Gryphius, Vondel, and Abraham a Sancta Clara. In the baroque age the great writers are also great Christians.

The same cannot be said of the eighteenth century, whose great writers are no longer Christians and indeed often opposed to Christianity: Voltaire, Rousseau, Swift, Fielding, Sterne, Lessing, Goethe, Schiller. In the age of Enlightenment Christianity no longer has a stake in world literature. Of course, there *is* Christian writing even in this rationalistic age, but no single religious work belongs to the great literary achievements of the age. Klopstock's *Messias* leans heavily on Milton's great epic. Martin von Cochem, Lavater, Tersteegen, Matthias Claudius, Jung-Stilling and Zinzendorf shine mildly in the literary firmament, but they are only tertiary stars. Hamann and Sailer act as powerful stimulants without themselves creating anything that belongs to world literature.

Outside Germany the state of Christian literature is still more melancholy. If we take a broad view we are forced to the conclusion that in the eighteenth century Christianity is not among the artistically productive forces.

This barren period makes the religious efflorescence of the nineteenth century all the more surprising. This efflorescence is reflected, as in the seventeenth century, in literary creations of the first rank. Professing Christians like Manzoni, Görres, Droste-Hülshoff, Newman, Kierkegaard, Dostoevsky and Hopkins are literary stars of the first magnitude. It is true that the situation is different from that prevailing in the seventeenth century, when faith was still strong, in that after the age of Enlightenment European civilization to a large extent bears the stamp of non-Christian and anti-Christian forces. While the Christian author of the baroque age could still count on the sympathy of a largely Christian reading public, the Christian writer of the nineteenth century (and twentieth) is faced by an unbelieving society whose materialism, liberalism and atheism must be taken into account. Again, the Christian writers of the baroque age were the products of a strong religious tradition, while those of the nineteenth century almost all came from the realm of unbelief, which they only succeeded in leaving behind after a mental and spiritual struggle. Before Chateaubriand, Lamennais, Lacordaire, Manzoni, Görres, Dostoevsky, Bloy and Péguy became ardent defenders of Christianity they were free-thinkers. Both Brentano and Kierkegaard lost their faith at certain periods in their lives. Newman, Faber, Hopkins, Thompson and Soloviev were converts, and so are, in the twentieth century, Haecker,

Le Fort, Bergengruen, Schaper, Döblin, Reinhold Schneider, Chesterton, Eliot, Greene, Waugh, Undset, Jörgensen, Claudel, Marcel and Papini. It almost seems as if spirits which have first passed through unbelief and error are best equipped to remind a nihilistic world of the truth of Christianity, for they know from their own experience the thoughts and feelings of those to whom they speak.

As for the Christian content of the nineteenth-century religious writer, it does not seem to be as strong in the Romantics, who are children of the eighteenth century, as in the religious writers and thinkers of the second half of the century. But one thing cannot fail to strike us about the period in which Gezelle was writing in Belgium, Dostoevsky and Soloviev in Russia, Newman, Hopkins and Thompson in England, and Péguy, Bloy and Claudel in France: in all those years (1848 to 1917) Germany did not produce one single work of Christian literature of the first rank.

CHAPTER I

THE SIXTEENTH CENTURY

THOMAS MORE (1478-1535)

Few great books have been so misunderstood as *Utopia*, which brought sudden fame throughout Europe to Thomas More, the great lawyer, diplomat and statesman. Written in the form of a dialogue, it describes political conditions on the island of "Nowhere". Its full title is: *"A most pleasant, fruitful and witty Work of the best State of a Public Weal, and the new Isle called Utopia."* It is neither a treatise nor a novel, but a satire. More was always ready for a joke, and as a young man wrote comedies, gay occasional verse and witty epigrams. His fondness for humour, satire and irony was universally known, and Erasmus said expressly of *Utopia* that More's intention was to make his friends laugh. We are also told that in his conversation More had the habit of making serious remarks with a smile and jokes in a serious tone. This habit may also have led astray the interpreters of *Utopia*: jokes have been taken in earnest, mature convictions as light-hearted trifling. So in the eighteenth century *Utopia* became the handbook of deists and rationalist political thinkers, in the nineteenth that of radicals and liberals, and in the twentieth that of communists and imperialists. But St Thomas More is by no means the spiritual progenitor of these unchristian ideologies; there is no contradiction between his *Utopia* and his religious writings. Immediately before *Utopia* he wrote the *Life of Pico*, a layman who united piety with erudition and was the youthful More's model. In *Utopia* More has made his Christianity just as plain. To be sure, the Utopian state is not Christian, but then it is not More's ideal state.

More puts the description of the Utopian state into the mouth of an interlocutor, Raphael Hythloday (that is, speaker of empty things, gossip). The irony implicit in this figure has often been overlooked. Hythloday is depicted as a fanatical theorist who takes no account of reality. Above all, he forgets that human nature was impaired by original sin. He believes that man is completely good and completely reasonable, and on this illusion he builds the conception of his communistic authoritarian State, which he himself involuntarily reduces to absurdity. The Christian realist More, who appears under his own name as the opponent of the non-Christian dreamer Hythloday, smilingly rejects this Utopia, which in reality exists "nowhere" and never could.

More

values man highly enough to believe him capable of good; but he does not trust him so much as to believe him capable only of good. . . . Human life is a web of light and dark . . . and therefore Thomas More fundamentally rejects a political conception like that of Hythloday, without being blind to all that is good and desirable in his dreams. But these good things appear in a context which is at variance with the reality of the world and of man as the Christian sees them. More not only leads us to points where these dreams descend into the ridiculous; he also shows us how close such self-deception can come to the dangerous and the inhuman. . . . With extraordinary perspicacity he has disclosed the illusions that appear when man thinks and acts without taking into account the limits of humanity (from a Christian point of view, human weakness and sinfulness).

(Möbus.)

More emphasizes that the state of Utopia is based on natural reason alone and is unillumined by the light of divine revelation. He wishes to show, "with an ironical side-glance at the present, how even a non-Christian community, with the help of mere reason, can solve many problems better than modern European statesmen, who should reflect on this and adopt what is useful; and how, on the other hand, reliance on reason alone unaccompanied by the true faith can easily lead to imperfections, foolishness and absurdity" (Brie). The author's purpose is to throw into relief, by contrast with a heathen State, that is in many respects excellent, the glaring injustices of so-called "Christian" States. "More did not mean to imply that paganism was better than Christianity. He meant to point out that many Christians were worse than pagans" (Chambers). *Utopia* was a protest against emerging individualism, the autocratic ways of the rich, the thievish policies of princes, mad wars and the despotism of the totalitarian State. In his *History of Richard III*, which had considerable influence on Shakespeare, he had already attacked the immoral power of the State in the early sixteenth century and anticipated, from the opposite point of view, Machiavelli's picture of the prince. He continued this attack against the Tudor tyranny still more brilliantly in *Utopia*. Almost everything that Henry VIII did later is here portrayed and condemned.

If More foresaw these dangerous developments, the reader may ask, why did he nevertheless enter Henry's service soon after the completion of the book? The answer is contained in *Utopia* itself. In it More says, like Plato, that States will only be happy when philosophers become kings or kings philosophers. As this is so far not the case, philosophers must at any rate advise kings. More admits that for sensible advice one can expect little thanks and that the advice is not followed either. "But you must not for this reason leave the commonwealth in the lurch. You cannot leave the ship in a storm just because you cannot steer it or control the winds. . . . Rather must you take care so to order what you cannot turn to good that it does not become worse. For it is impossible for everything on earth to be good unless all men were to be good." More took a sober view of what was politically possible, but he also saw that we had a duty to be active within those limits. That is the Christian attitude to politics.

At no point in his career did More fail to make a cool appraisal of his position; he always displayed a superior calmness of mind. At the height of his good fortune he wrote his grimmest book, *The Four Last Things*. In it he says:

> For some of the old famous philosophers, when they were demanded what faculty philosophy was, answered that it was the meditation or exercise of death. . . . Now if this be the whole study and labour of philosophy, as the best philosophers said that it is, then may we within short time be well learned in philosophy . . . for if we stop to think, the world is a prison, and I myself am a prisoner condemned to death, which I cannot escape. . . . Therefore no reasonable man will think more highly of himself because he has office or power in this world; he is no more than a prisoner whom the chief gaoler has set over his fellow-prisoners, until the executioner's cart comes for him too.

In spite of the emphasis it lays on the authority of the State, *Utopia* itself had left no doubt that there are bounds to this authority. There are things which the State cannot command. Holy as the laws of the State are, there are laws which stand above the State. Among them are man's right and freedom not to be compelled to say something that he does not believe. More admits that this is a lowly concept of freedom, but he held fast to it to the end. Even this lowly concept of freedom he was only able to realize at the cost of his life. When he refused to swear an oath denying the spiritual authority of the pope, Henry VIII had his Lord Chancellor thrown into the Tower and finally beheaded.

The books which this brave man wrote in prison are more carefree and gay than anything he wrote when he was free. What a difference there is between the dark treatise on *The Four Last Things,* written at the summit of good fortune, and the cheerful *Dialogue of Comfort*, written in a dungeon! It is a dialogue between a pious and humorous Hungarian nobleman and his weak nephew on the question of the attitude to be adopted in face of the conquest of the country by the Turks. The parallel between Henry VIII and the Turks is obvious. John the Baptist, too, was beheaded by a tyrant. "And now sitteth he, with great feast in heaven, at God's board. . . . Now to this great glory can there no man come headless. Our head is Christ: and therefore to him must we be joined, and as members of his must we follow him. . . . Knew you not that Christ must suffer passion, and by that way enter into his kingdom? Who can for very shame desire to enter into the Kingdom of Christ with ease, when himself entered not into his own without pain?"

In preparation for his own end, which was approaching inexorably, the prisoner wrote the *Treatise on the Passion*. More hears Christ speak to those who, like himself, are full of anxiety: "Take courage, weak heart! Even if you are nervous, sad and tired, and tremble before the most painful tortures, be comforted! For I have conquered the whole world, yet I felt far more fear, grief and tiredness and also far more mental insecurity when I saw my bitterest suffering coming upon me so swiftly. He who is of good courage can find a thousand brave and glorious martyrs, whose example he can follow joyfully. But you, weak, trembling, foolish sheep, must think it enough to walk behind me, who am your shepherd and guide; if you distrust yourself, you can put all your trust in me. Grasp the hem of my garment; from it you will draw strength and help to go on."

The *Meditations*, which More wrote in the Tower on the blank pages of a book of Hours, are full of the same spirit. They are simple, clear requests like this one: "Give me the grace, good Lord, to despise the world, to fix my mind firmly on you and not to let myself be dependent on the breath of human mouth." But the finest evidence of the unshakable firmness and unquenchable cheerfulness of this Christian Socrates is to be found in his *Letters from Prison*. The majority are addressed to his favourite daughter, Meg. Often written in charcoal on scraps of paper, while he was worried by rats and disease, they emit a wonderful radiance: "Thank God, my mind is at peace and I desire no more worldly possessions than I have. I beg him to make you all joyful in the hope of heaven. . . . Probably those who have put me in here believe that they have done something very unpleasant to me. But I assure you that, had I not a wife and children, I should long ago have retired to a still smaller space. . . . I feel as though God had made me his favourite, put me on his knee and fondled me.'

The speech that More made to his judges after they had condemned him to death is a classic: "This verdict is based on a law of Parliament that is clear contrary to the laws of God and of his holy Church. No worldly prince can arrogate to himself by any law the supreme guidance of the Church or of a part of the Church, for it rightfully belongs to the Bishop of Rome." More bases his case on the Bible, the Fathers and the whole Christian tradition. Just as a town can make no law that is contrary to the laws of the whole country, so a country can make no law against the whole of Christendom. "Therefore I am not bound to direct my conscience according to the council of one single kingdom against the general council of Christendom. For on my side I have over a hundred of the aforementioned holy bishops against every bishop of yours, on my side all the councils of the last thousand years against one council or parliament of yours (and God knows what sort of parliament), on my side all other Christian countries against this one kingdom." More spoke in the consciousness that Christianity is not a national, but an international matter. As a martyr of the universal Catholic Church he has lived on in the memory of posterity. The oldest biographies of him, those of William Roper and Nicholas Harpsfield, became themselves valuable contributions to Christian literature and continue to move and edify numberless readers today. The *Life of More* by Roper, the saint's son-in-law, has been called by an expert "perhaps the most perfect small biography in the English language" (Chambers).

MARTIN LUTHER (1483–1546)

The man against whom More wrote a polemical pamphlet was opposed to him in other things besides religion. Luther and More were also complete opposites in temperament and character. The stormy German reformer was very different from the polished English humanist. Yet they were both deeply religious men who took the voice of conscience very seriously. But conscience made one of them a martyr *for* the papacy and the other a rebel *against* it.

Luther's literary work sprang from his zeal for reform. Everything he wrote—the *Fables from Aesop*, the polemical writings, the translation of the Bible, the hymns—was intended to contribute to the religious education of the people. The literary and also "the religious masterpiece of Luther" (Lortz) was his translation of the Scriptures into German. In conformity with the Augustinian rule, when he was a monk he had soaked himself in the Bible. His translation into German is not the first, but in literary power it surpasses all its predecessors. "No one before or after him has rendered so vividly the living intensity of the Word of God" (Lortz). It cannot be denied, however, that his own subjectivity has entered into the translation; we cannot help being struck by the distinction between essential and inessential books of Scripture and the disregard for the Epistle of St James and the Apocalypse in a man who made the Bible the only criterion of faith and said of his opponents: "They should respect the Word of God." Nevertheless, the language of Luther's Bible influenced Catholics as well. For example, Hieronymus Emser based his translation of the New Testament on Luther's work. The development of the German language and of German literature is inseparably linked with Luther's Bible.

The reformer was also a pioneer as a hymn-writer, although he was not the first in this field either. There had been German hymns in the centuries before him, and he himself took over and remodelled some of them. He drew abundantly on Catholic tradition; his thirty-seven hymns are for the most part adaptations of psalms, and Latin hymns and sequences of the old Church. They remould what had been handed down by tradition into a new form that the people could understand. Luther's hymns "express in their whole conception the idea of communal prayer. . . . . This idea of divine service is still nourished by the objectivity of the liturgical singing of the Catholic past. With this attitude the community sings the German versions of the psalms and hymns as chorales. Luther's hymns are far removed from the personal hymns of Pietism. They still live, like Luther's faith, on the abundance of the facts of salvation" (Lortz).

In form they often achieve tremendous force. A good example is *Ein' feste Burg ist unser Gott*, which is based on Psalm 46. It contains such powerful phrases as "der alt' böse Feind",[1] which by piling up heavily accented syllables has an exceptionally concentrated effect. Carlyle rightly says of this hymn: "There is something about it like the roar of an avalanche or the first crash of an earthquake. In the very force of the dissonance is revealed a higher harmony." The text contains attractive rallying-cries like "Though the world were full of devils . . . we shall yet succeed", and "They shall let the Word abide". Luther's hymns are sermons, battle-cries and confessions of faith all rolled into one. That Luther is also capable of striking a more intimate note is shown by hymns like *Nun freut euch lieben Christen gmein Und lasst uns fröhlich springen*,[2] one of his few completely original compositions and one that gives characteristic testimony of his faith. Here, too, Christ fights for Man against the Devil. But the tone of the *Minnelied*, the love-song, becomes perceptible in these words about Christ:

> Er sprach zu mir: Halt dich an mich,
> Es soll dir itzt gelingen,
> Ich geb mich selber gang für dich,
> Da will ich für dich ringen,
> Denn ich bin dein und du bist mein,
> Und wo ich bleib, da soltu sein,
> Uns soll der Feind nicht scheiden.[3]

[1] "The old wicked enemy."

[2] "Now rejoice all Christians together and let us leap for joy."

[3] "He said to me: Hold on to me, now shall you succeed; I give myself completely for you, and I shall wrestle for you, for I am yours and you are mine, and where I am, there shall you be, and the foe shall not part us."

"The often-posed question whether Luther was at heart a poet, or whether he was a man of many gifts who forced himself to write a few hymns and hymn-tunes because of his position and calling" is answered by the poet R. A. Schröder with the simple statement, "He was a poet". It is quite certain that Luther had an intuitive understanding of language, and this enabled him to become the founder of the Protestant hymn. His example was contagious: there was soon an abundance of evangelical hymn-books, and Catholic hymn-books, modelled on them, appeared, too. The evangelical hymn retained its leading position, for, being an essential part of the liturgy, it was far more intensely cultivated than the Catholic German hymn, which never achieved liturgical rank.

In this connection it deserves to be mentioned that Luther's folksong-like *Vom Himmel hoch, da komm ich her* ("From heaven on high I come") was taken over by Catholic hymn-books and is still sung in Catholic churches today, with an additional verse, *Es kam ein Engel hell und klar* ("There came an angel bright and clear"). Altogether an amazingly large number of hymns soon became the common property of both Churches.

IGNATIUS OF LOYOLA (1491–1556)

The founder of Protestantism was a man of action and at the same time a born writer; the founder of the Society of Jesus can lay no claim to possess this double gift. The Basque Ignatius of Loyola was fundamentally an unliterary man. Yet his autobiography, his *Spiritual Exercises* and his letters belong to world literature. What he wrote was written in the service of his world-wide activity; that is what gave it its tremendous force and long-lasting influence.

Ignatius in the last years of his life dictated his *Reminiscences* of the time from 1521 to 1540 to a Jesuit father. In this he describes in the third person his spiritual development from the dissolute soldier into the saint: the wound he received in

the fortress of Pamplona, his recovery and conversion at the
castle of Loyola, his penance at Manresa, his pilgrimage to
Jerusalem, his studies in various towns in Spain and in Paris,
the vow he made with his first companions in Montmartre, the
apostolic work in Italy, his settling in Rome, the confirmation
of the Society of Jesus by the pope—these were the stages on
his path. This path led at first from one extreme to the other,
which was not surprising in a man who had no time for half-
measures. It was only the collision with reality and the illumination of grace that with the years put everything into pro-
portion.

Grace was already at work at Manresa. Ignatius tells us how
he sat down one day on the bank of the River Cardona and
looked into the water.

> Then the eyes of his spirit began to open. It was not that he
> had seen a vision, but he was granted knowledge and under-
> standing of many things concerning the spiritual life, and con-
> cerning faith and theology. This was accompanied by such
> great illumination that everything seemed new to him. It is
> impossible to indicate in detail what he then understood. The
> only thing that can be said is that he received great clarity of
> mind. If he adds all the helping graces he has received from
> God in the sixty-two years of his life to what he already knew
> then, he considers all this less than what he received on that
> single occasion. That experience was so impressive that his
> spirit remained as it were illumined. He felt as if he had become
> a different person.

From then onwards he worried not only about his own
salvation but also about the salvation of others. For their sake
he wrote down his own experiences and knowledge, and so
there came into being at Manresa one of the most remarkable
books in the world, the book of exercises.

Ignatius calls his book *Spiritual Exercises* "intended to help
the reader to conquer himself and to arrange his life so that it
is not governed by uncontrolled inclinations". The exercises
are based on the question of man's goal. "Man is created to

praise, honour and serve God, his Lord, and by so doing to save his soul. Whatever else there is on earth is created for man's sake; it is there to help him to reach his goal. It follows that man must use it in so far as it helps him to attain his goal, and abstain from it in so far as it hinders him."

The suggestions in the *Exercises* are not intended just to be read but to be carried out under the guidance of an experienced priest, so that a man makes up his mind to let God govern his life. Moved by the force of insight, the will of the person practising the exercises is to be completely converted. In the imitation of Christ man, once freed from the fetters of sin, is supposed to attain the freedom of the children of God. Through his own knowledge of men Ignatius knew that the purely rational knowledge of abstract truths cannot accomplish this conversion. Only truths emotionally experienced as concrete realities can impart the decisive direction to the will. So the *Spiritual Exercises* appeal not only to the reason but also very strongly to the imagination.

The triple shape of sin is displayed in dramatic pictures: the fall of the angels is depicted as a fall into hell, the fall of the first man as exile from paradise, and the fall of the individual as a plunge into the abyss. The angels, the saints and finally God himself appear before the contrite sinner and disclose the full horror of his sin. Repetitions deepen sorrow and inflame imagination in order to introduce a still more powerful experience: the curtain is torn aside to disclose a view of hell: the sinner sees the fire, hears the screams of the damned, smells smoke and sulphur, tastes the tears and feels the flames. Finally Christ appears to him, bodily present on the cross, and forces him to ask: "What have I done for thee until now? What else am I to do?"

The second week comforts the sinner, who has been ground to pieces under the weight of his sins, with the sight of the divine glory. He experiences the birth of Christ and the homage of the three kings as a tangible reality. Then Christ, the best of emperors, raises his standard against the standard of Lucifer.

The aspirant must decide between Satan on his throne in Babylon and Christ on a hill outside Jerusalem. The possibilities of choice in everyday life are given concrete form. Worldly goods are to be no further hindrance to serving God.

The third week strengthens the decision that has been taken. Once again the penitent lives through the sufferings of Christ; he feels the cuts of the scourge and the nails in his flesh. But the resolution he has made protects him. Suffering has roused him to action and he can thus overcome it. Again sorrow leads to joy: in the last week the converted sinner hears the rejoicings of the resurrection. Henceforth his actions are ruled by unconditional obedience to God.

The *Spiritual Exercises* strongly influenced the history of ideas. They had a direct effect on the content and tenor of the Catholic hymn and on the Jesuit drama of the seventeenth century. And, what is more important, they put a decisive stamp on the lives of thousands.

We are given a glimpse into the character of St Ignatius by the seven thousand *Letters* which have come down to us. Among them we find, in Spanish, Italian and Latin, letters to popes and cardinals about Church reform, letters to kings and to the great about politics, letters to his followers about matters concerning the Society, and letters dealing with the manifold questions in which high and low, men and women turned trustfully to him for advice. These letters are the work of a psychologist wise in the ways of the world, who could move in every layer of society with easy confidence. Ignatius was very clever, but he was not what many people mean by the term "clever Jesuit". He loved frankness and openness. Any kind of secrecy, duplicity or slyness was hateful to him. He fought with his vizor open, for he had nothing to hide. Such openness is only possible to a man who has himself completely under control. Ignatius possessed this self-control. You can see it clearly in his letters. They preserve a discreet distance from people and things, refrain from any kind of exaggeration and are almost dry in their polite moderation. This manly and astringent spirit could not chatter so delightfully in his letters as the great Teresa. He was reticent by nature. But behind the outward coolness the reader can divine a loving heart with a wonderful gift for "grasping and understanding the peculiarities of others" (Karrer). Loyola's capacity for identification is more than a tactical, diplomatic sympathy; it is rooted in Christian love, which loves and respects a fellow-being for God's sake.

Ignatius's piety has been aptly described as "worldly mysticism" (K. Rahner). For it enabled the saint, in a deeper sense than the worldly people of the Renaissance, to accept with joy the things of this world: not as opportunities for enjoyment, but as means of praising God. Praying is only *one* way of praising God. Faithful work pleases God no less. We should not strive after pleasant hours of devotion, but "find God in every kind of task and bring to life the spirit of devotion in all we do". Everything is prayer for him who does everything "for the greater service of God. . . . There is unquestionably more virtue and grace in being able to rejoice in God in various tasks and in various places rather than in just one, the prie-dieu." Man must be ready to serve God in this way or that, without any thought for himself, indifferent to everything created, with his eye always fixed on the goal of all creation. In this way he becomes a pliable tool "for the greater glory of God". "Preserve in everything freedom of mind. Never spare a thought for what men may think, but always keep your mind so free inwardly that you could always do the opposite."

Besides an unbounded trust in divine grace, Ignatius also had great trust in human nature: "When I look to the Lord God in everything and how to please him, I should consider it an error to rely on human means and efforts. On the other hand, I cannot consider it safe to stake everything on trust in God and not bestir myself and use the natural means which he has put in my hand. Rather am I convinced, under God, that I should do the one thing and not neglect the other, as long as I always have the greater glory of God—and nothing else—

in view." One of the most important natural means is good health. Again and again Ignatius used to warn his brothers against exaggerated asceticism: "Many things are lost by lack of moderation: bodily health, mental vigour, an example for our neighbour to imitate, God's glory." To Francis Borgia he wrote:

So far as fasting and abstinence are concerned, I am in favour of your keeping your bodily powers healthy for the service of the Lord; you should strengthen them, not weaken them. . . . Instead of weakening oneself by immoderate self-chastisement, it is more sensible to honour God by spiritual acts and other moderate exercises. Then not only will the soul be at peace, a healthy spirit will also dwell in a healthy body and the whole man will be healthier and better equipped to serve God.

In the very earliest letter that has come down to us from Ignatius he says:

The Lord does not require of you things which bring you too heavy a burden or can do you harm; on the contrary, he likes to see you walk in joy before his face, and you are not to deny even the body its needs. Remain always at one with him not only in spirit, but also in thought, word and deed; and in the outward affairs to which you have to attend think above all of doing God's will! He expects that from us; indeed, it is his command. [The saint wished] to find God in everything, to love him in everything and everything in him. . . . When a man has left himself behind and entered into his creator and Lord, ever full of joy that our eternal good lies in everything created, there is happiness beyond compare for him. For to those who love our Lord, all things are offered as aids to come nearer . . . to their Creator and Lord.

VITTORIA COLONNA (1490–1547)

One of the most enlightened women with whom Ignatius of Loyola corresponded was Vittoria Colonna, Countess of Pescara. The widow of the famous imperial general was one of the pillars of the Catholic reform movement. She was respected by the pope and the emperor, and influential cardinals were her friends. Her intellect and virtue were admired by Ariosto and beloved by Michelangelo. In the age of the Renaissance she was "the most famous lady in Italy . . . immortal as a poetess . . . a saint" (J. Burckhardt). "Without a knowledge of Vittoria's life and writings the character of the Catholic reform in the sixteenth century cannot be fully comprehended" (Reumont). Her noble lyric poems rank among the pearls of world literature and the most perfect expression of Christian piety.

After her husband's early death she composed over a hundred sonnets and canzonets dedicated to his memory. At first it seems that her grief will never end. Again and again the lonely widow breaks out into the loving cry, "You were my sun!" But the discipline imposed on her by the strict sonnet-form gradually became the means of controlling and purifying her grief. These poems have rightly been called "stages along a path on which Vittoria learnt to drink from the chalice of death a higher kind of life" (Gertrud Bäumer). In one of the sonnets we meet these lines:

Thus there grows from my deepest sorrow—his death—
The fruit of faith, the soul's daily bread.

Again in another sonnet she says: "So I exchange my grief for eternal bliss and strive ever upward. All at once the ray of God's grace strikes me with heavenly fire." The end of this inner transformation is marked by the last of the poems mourning her husband. It is a madrigal:

You long and pine and grieve,
You rejoice and are then ashamed
And in your greed your heart is only heavier.
You wanted to snatch and see too much—
And in the end your heart is only emptier!
Then suddenly you learn to understand:
Your sorrow passes,
Joy takes its place:
Light in all its glory floods through all your
Being—you know the truth.

She has finally emerged from the miasma of grief. Hence-forth, illumined by an inner light, she has only one aim: to sanctify her life by the imitation of Christ. The experience of salvation takes such a hold on her that in the second period of her life it becomes almost the only subject of her poetry. Just as she once celebrated her earthly love in the image of the sun, so now the same image represents the divine power, by which she feels herself sustained. As Gertrud Bäumer says:

> Her poetry is an image of the true religious life through the rise and fall of the ceaseless longing from which the stars over the dark sea of earthly existence keep disappearing. It is pre-cisely this which makes Vittoria Colonna, for all the fervour of her piety, before which all other earthly matters pale into insignificance, seem so human. Her struggle often reaches titanic proportions; you can feel the fire of a mighty spirit struggling with God: I shall not leave you alone until you bless me. The great pictures of her native countryside rise up as symbols of the storm inside her:

> > See the heavens stirred by dark storm-clouds!
> > They roar and whirl through the air,
> > With thunder and lightning over mountain and ravine,
> > Trying to shatter the earth's hard crust.

So strongly does she feel the power of the great world-mover to crack the hardened soul, sweeping away in the storm what is withered and unfruitful, so that it opens up, purified and warmed, to bloom with fresh life. After such storms the har-monies of peace sound all the purer and more heartfelt. Her devotional poetry as a whole gives a unique picture of how a soul *lives* with the world of Christianity. One after the other the half-human, half-divine figures emerge as though from the shadows, bathed in the "eternal light" kindled in her soul. The surprising thing about these figures is the originality of their conception, which often abandons the framework of tradition. Quotation cannot convey the wealth of these spiritual lyrics; they are rich in original characterization, in depth of meaning, in range of devotion and feeling, in ripe thought, in the exhaust-ive use of symbolism and in the representational significance with which the sacred figures are endowed. Her hymns to Mary plumb the very depths of the natural as well as the religious life.

One of her loveliest poems is a sort of literary equivalent to a Pietà of Michelangelo:

> Her bosom heaved, for her arm embraced in sorrow the dead God, the son once born to her. She meditated. Her spirit already divined the triumph which he won before the most elect.

> She sat and thought. His countenance began to fade. New, wild sorrow now sprang from her breast. But again his eternal kingdom, his goal, rose victoriously, full of glory.

> For she learnt, secretly from the mouth of God, that he was not dead, but only given into death's keeping until the hour of resurrection.

> Yet as his own true mother, although she knew him in his glory, she was quite without comfort until the last hour.

The Spiritual Poems of her last years, which are devoted to the sufferings of Christ in Gethsemane and on Golgotha, are full of comfort in spite of their gentle melancholy. "The sorrow and imperfection of all earthly activity are now washed away for Vittoria in the sphere of heavenly harmonies" (Pfister).

TERESA OF AVILA (1515–82)

Like Vittoria' Colonna, Teresa, too, is of noble lineage, an important Catholic reformer and the greatest woman writer in the classical literature of her country; but in range and depth of mind the Italian is far surpassed by the overwhelming personality of the gifted Spaniard. Teresa is one of the greatest saints in the whole history of the Church, and her works "must be reckoned among the world's greatest literature" (Julius Langbehn).

Teresa's first literary effort was inspired by the popular romances of chivalry like *Amadis*, which dealt with fighting and love. She devoured this exciting reading hungrily, and herself wrote one of these romantic novels full of fantastic adventures. How after long spiritual turmoil she turned from a vain and empty-headed girl into a nun of heroic piety Teresa herself has described in detail in her autobiography. Self-descriptions are usually not distinguished by their fondness for truth; Teresa's frank autobiography is an exception. It is particularly important because it shows that holiness in a human being is not present from the beginning, but must be attained by painful striving. Teresa had already lived for twenty years in a convent before she reached the stage of living only for God. The way was full of defeats and disappointments. But he who uses force wins heaven for himself—if he trusts to grace. It was not for nothing that Teresa called the story of her life *The Book of God's Mercies*. By this title she wanted to make it clear that in the mystical life God is the active partner; the soul on its own can do nothing but keep itself strictly disciplined.

What a steep ascent Teresa made is disclosed by her books on mysticism: *The Way of Perfection*, an introduction to inward prayer for nuns, and above all *The Interior Castle*, a systematic portrayal of the mystical experience. It was not out of conceit but on the orders of her confessors and superiors, and with the aim of helping others, that she described her experiences in the spiritual life. Anyone who understands by mysticism something dark, misty, vague and unhealthily emotional should read these books; he will be surprised by their clarity and healthy tone. Teresa was by no means uncritical about her mystical experiences: "Certainly no woman has delineated these experiences with such exactness and self-control, or made the language so transparently clear, as she whose testimony incontestably revealed that mysticism is a reality" (Reinhold Schneider). Teresa treated the visions and ecstasies as inessential, and she never regarded these exceptional states as more valuable than the normal prayer of the simple Christian. The real essence of mysticism is nothing more than what forms the kernel of all devotion, even if it appears in mysticism in a particularly intensive form: namely the effort at all times to unite the human will completely with the divine will. That is the mark of holiness: to do God's will, even if our own will strives in another direction: "The highest degree of perfection obviously does not lie in . . . sublime ecstasies or even in visions . . ., but only in such uniformity of our own will with God's, that we embrace everything that we recognize as his will with our own whole will, and accept the bitter and the painful, when we recognize that it is God's will, as joyfully as the pleasant."

The amazing thing about Teresa is the fact that she by no means led an exclusively contemplative life behind the walls of her convent, but on the contrary was tremendously active. In the teeth of wide opposition and under indescribable difficulties this masculine woman reformed the Carmelite Order and founded seventeen convents. We still possess today, in her 450 lively letters and her delightful book of *Foundations*, a colourful, living and often dramatic picture of this ceaseless activity. Her fresh, colloquial style, whose easy volubility puts the reader under a spell, brings events to life before our eyes. We see this mystic planning new foundations, acquiring plots of land, negotiating with spiritual and temporal authorities, solving financial problems, building houses, choosing prioresses, making clothes and building churches. In all these activities she displays a wonderful talent for organization and considerable skill in diplomacy; she overcomes all resistance, sometimes with humour, at others with a steely resolution. All her actions are accompanied by wonderful confidence. Teresa trusts blindly in God. For this reason she can approach the great quite unafraid, and even in her letters to King Philip II she does not mince her words. Nor does she fear the Devil: "I don't care two straws about devils! They don't worry me any more than flies. It is they who must fear me! I don't understand how people can be frightened of them. How can they say 'Satan, Satan!' We can always say 'God, God', so that they tremble." Teresa made no concessions over essentials: "No one will ever win anything from me if I see that it is against my conscience, even if it brings the world down in ruins." She was a fighter by nature: "It is certain that there is no complete security anywhere in this life, and we can never consider ourselves safe; for we are continually at war and surrounded by many enemies."

Her zeal for reform was far removed from fanaticism. Teresa wrote expressly against excessive strictness in the striving after perfection. Wherever she noticed that a nun was inclined to exaggerated self-chastisement, she ordered another sensible sister to keep a watch on her and to forbid any excesses. To a prioress she wrote: "Look after your health; for it is better to look after yourself properly than to be ill." For herself, it is true, she stuck to her watch-word: "Either suffer or die!" We often find in her letters sentences like this one: "I promise you that I will pay no attention to my poor health. . . . We have nothing else to worry about but following him who lived continually in pain although he was quite innocent. . . . The Lord continually gives me bad health, and when in spite of it I can do everything I sometimes have to laugh." Her powers of endurance were indeed amazing. In spite of her manifold maladies this brave woman was often travelling in order to set new foundations on their feet or to visit convents. Nothing would damp her cheerfulness. For her, death had lost its terrors. When a nun died, she forbade mourning and composed joyful hymns for the sisters to sing by the coffin. She rejoiced that Sister Beatrice "has died such a holy death and entered on eternal rest. I can only wonder how people can mourn over such great good fortune. Should we not rather envy the departed?" She wanted to see her convents filled with this joy, which does not cease even in the face of death. She did not care for melancholy nuns: "I am more frightened of a discontented nun than of a host of evil spirits." Melancholy people were not to be accepted: "God preserve me from saints with irritable expressions."

Teresa's love of nature is striking. In her letters she often expresses her joy in a beautiful view and her preference for flowing water. She says to a prioress: "Do you think it unimportant to be in a convent from which the ships on the river can be seen? It is a great help in the praise of the Lord." Teresa knows from experience: "To me it was useful to be able to see fields, water or flowers. These things inspired me and helped me to collect my thoughts." The sights of nature are for her symbols of the supernatural life: a garden in bloom is the symbol of the soul, in which virtues sprout and give fragrance; and water means grace, which irrigates the parched earth and makes it fruitful. Every time of drought increases the burning thirst for the life-giving flood. Teresa's mind was broad enough to embrace earthly as well as heavenly things. Her piety has nothing gloomy or narrow-minded about it; on the contrary, it breathes joy in everything. She could feel God's presence everywhere: "My daughters, remember that God is near to you even in the kitchen among the pots." The secret of the wonderful harmony of her many-sided personality lies in the words with which she used to strengthen herself: "Nothing shall worry you, nothing shall frighten you. Everything passes. God alone remains the same. Patience accomplishes everything. He who possesses God can lack nothing. God alone is enough."

The originality of Teresa's writings gave them unparalleled influence on the spiritual life of Europe. "Without them the sixteenth century would be incomplete and modern Catholic devotion incomprehensible" (Lortz). French mysticism and the religious achievements of the seventeenth century stood under her aegis. Francis de Sales, Fénelon, Libuori and Sailer all admired Teresa and learnt from her. Even in the non-Catholic world her influence lasted for centuries after her death. Johann Arndt, an important Protestant theologian and writer, was strongly influenced by her. Thomasius, one of the leaders of the German Enlightenment, made a profound study of her work. Gottfried Arnold, one of the leading Pietists, translated Teresa's writings. Tersteegen, the Protestant poet and mystic from the Lower Rhine, wrote an enthusiastic biography of her. The philosopher Leibniz looked up to her with respect, and admitted that she had stimulated his thinking. The Protestant poet Crashaw, one of the greatest baroque lyric poets England produced, was led by Teresa's writings to Catholicism and the priesthood. Macaulay called Teresa, in one of his famous essays, "the heart of the Catholic reform movement", and declared that she belonged to humanity as a whole. The Freiherr von Stein, a real old-fashioned Lutheran, recommended his daughters to read St Teresa. In our day Victoria Sackville-West has written a life of St Teresa and has described her as "one of the most gifted women who have ever lived". The Jewish philosopher Edith Stein was so inspired by the figure of Teresa that she became a convert and entered Carmel. The Protestant theologian Walter Rigg devoted two admiring essays to the saint. He calls her "one of the greatest women in history. . . . No words of praise can do her justice, for there is scarcely a comparison that she cannot support. . . . It is remarkable that we read Dostoevsky and Kafka, Pascal and Kierkegaard, and we are right to do so. But why do we not soak ourselves in the writings of Teresa? A really Christian outlook is hardly possible without them."

JOHN OF THE CROSS (1542–91)

St Teresa of Avila's friend and her colleague in the reform of the Carmelite Order is also one of the classics of Spanish literature. John of the Cross wrote poetry of magical beauty, and his prose is musical in its rhythms. In spite of this he is not an easily accessible writer, for he was extremely reserved by nature, his mysticism is of a somewhat special kind, and his works are almost untranslatable; they only reveal their full beauty in the original Spanish. Walter Rigg also points to another reason which makes him difficult to understand: John of the Cross is a great saint and at the same time a great artist, "the poet among saints and the saint among poets. His experience is a poetic one. . . . He is a genuinely religious poet, for whom writing a poem is a sacramental activity." It is precisely this which makes him so difficult of access: "The literary expert usually lacks the religious sense to understand him, while the religious person often lacks the taste for literature" (Rigg). To appreciate John of the Cross at his true worth, one must be a discriminating judge of poetry and at the same time a theologian with some experience of the mystical life.

It might be supposed that the work of a man who was at the same time a mystic and a poet would be highly subjective. With John of the Cross the opposite is the case: "Although his work contains the most intimate personal experience it is completely impersonal; he does not speak of himself and of his own life, but only of the unfathomable space in which the soul approaches God to be grasped and raised up by him. . . . He had only one experience to convey: the ascent that turns into a process of being carried aloft, the flight of the bird that at a certain altitude is taken on to the wings of a greater one and carried straight into the Light" (Reinhold Schneider). Everything that John of the Cross wrote centres exclusively round the two poles of God and the soul. It shows how the soul takes the upward path to God: in steps, from purification through illumination to unification. It is a steep and dangerous path, which leads past sinister abysses but also provides dazzling views of vertiginous peaks. The purgative way is described particularly in *The Ascent of Mount Carmel* and *The Dark Night of the Soul,* the illuminative way in *The Spiritual Canticle* and the unitive way in *The Living Flame of Love.* Thus the major works of John of the Cross form a complete system of mystical theology.

His poems were the fruit of indescribable suffering. They sprang from his heart in the gloom and pain of months of imprisonment and desperate loneliness. They were not verses of complaint or accusation but of the purest joy. "Seldom has such a black situation produced such sheer jubilation" (Rigg). This lyrical poetry is the foundation of his splendid prose works. They are all explanations of these joyful songs, commentaries intended to show the struggling seeker the way to these heights. Meticulously they explain his often enigmatic poems, line for line and word for word; not in the dry style of the philologist but in a way that is itself full of living poetry. These comprehensive prose commentaries are themselves a

34 THE SIXTEENTH CENTURY

part of world literature. Dante himself explained and interpreted his sonnets and canzonets in the *Vita nuova*, but John of the Cross goes far beyond this rational self-interpretation.

In the *Steps to Perfection* these words occur: "Never do or say anything that Christ would not do or say, too, if he were your age, held the same position in society and enjoyed the same state of health." Christ is the model, the goal and the source of the spiritual life. To win him presupposes complete renunciation of self: "If you wish to reach the stage of enjoying everything, then seek enjoyment in nothing. . . . If you wish to reach the stage of knowing everything, then seek to know nothing about anything. If you wish to attain to what you are not, then you must go where you are nothing." The soul must be cleansed and purified. Man must become empty, so that fullness can stream in. He must even suffer so that he can enter into eternal joy. "Suffering out of love of God is better than working miracles." From his own experience John knows the value of pain: "Desire nothing but the cross, and without comfort, for the cross is perfect in itself." In this view even abandonment by God, darkness and barrenness of soul gain a positive value. In the midst of darkness the mystic sees the divine light. He makes the great discovery that the night itself is light, that the divine light can only appear to us men as darkness. God is such dazzling light that he plunges our eyes into darkness: "The clearer and more evident divine things are in themselves, the darker and more hidden they must naturally be to the soul." The more the soul is veiled in darkness, the more light it receives.

After the painful and dark night a kind of divine awakening takes place, as John of the Cross describes in the *Living Flame of Love:*

> The soul is like some one waking up, who first draws a deep breath . . .; it is as if the soul said: "Thou, my divine bridegroom, awakenest in the centre of my soul, deep down where thou dwellest in secrecy and silence as its lord and master!" Here the prayer of the psalmist is heard: "Wake, Lord, why

sleepest thou?" [That means, as John of the Cross says:] Awake us, for we are asleep. Awake us, so that we can know and love the blessings which thou offerest to us unceasingly. . . . Herein lies the great joy of this awakening: it enables us to know creatures through God, not God through his creatures; the effects through their cause, not the cause through its effects.

At the highest stage of withdrawal from the world the soul turns to it again and sees it from God's point of view in a quite different light. A transfiguring glow is shed from Christ over the whole creation: as the Father saw things in the Son, he lent them through this vision a certain beauty, and the beauty was heightened by Christ's descent to earth and ascension into heaven. "Through the mystery of the incarnation of his Son and his glorious resurrection according to the flesh, the Father has not only lent creatures a certain beauty but has also left them clad, as it were, in the perfect raiment of glory and majesty" (*Spiritual Canticle*). This vision of the creation provides the poet with a wealth of images which alone enable him to put the ineffable into words. Thus the poet of God's beauty becomes also a poet of the beauty of nature. The dissolving of a drop of water in wine without the destruction of the drop's substance; the wedding of spotless glass with the light that falls through it, a wedding in which the glass still continues to exist; the kindling of air in the flame; the transformation of wood in fire; the sprig of olive that was grafted on to a wild olive and now grows green no longer from itself: all these things are symbols of the transformation of the soul by faith. John of the Cross does not even shrink from using the rapture and delight of sexual love as symbols of the sweet intoxication of the love in which the soul and Christ find each other. The language of sexual and erotic imagery even becomes in his hands the best means of expressing the highest stage in the spiritual life, the union in the mystical marriage. In this he follows the tradition of the wedding-song and medieval bridal mysticism. In his commentary on the *Spiritual Canticle* John of the Cross explains the meaning of the mystic marriage:

It consists in a complete transformation of the lovers' souls, in which both, the Son of God and the soul, surrender in complete reciprocal possession of each other, through a sort of consummation of the union. By this means the soul is deified, and even shares in God, so far as that is possible here on earth. . . . This union cannot take place fully in this life, but it surpasses anything that can be expressed in words or grasped by the intelligence.

John of the Cross has exerted incalculable influence on his order, on theology and on modern theological writing. He was rightly granted the title of Doctor of the Church. Gottfried Arnold's translation of his writings shows that he has had considerable influence outside the Catholic Church. It must be admitted that his work has never become popular. With his gentle but insistent voice, John of the Cross speaks to a spiritual and religious élite. His spirit lives again in poets like Hopkins, T. S. Eliot and Reinhold Schneider.

CHAPTER II

THE SEVENTEENTH CENTURY

SPAIN

Calderon (1600–81)

The tradition founded by Ignatius of Loyola, Teresa of Avila and John of the Cross lived on in Pedro Calderon de la Barca, who after being educated by the Jesuits became a scholar, a soldier and finally a priest, and as a poet carried Spanish literature to its highest point. He is supposed to have written more than 400 plays, of which 108 tragedies and comedies and 73 religious pieces have been preserved.

As Spain experienced neither a Reformation nor a Renaissance, Spanish baroque literature inherited without a break the legacy of the Middle Ages and was able to continue the tradition of the mystery and morality plays. While French, English and German drama, the child of the Renaissance and of humanism, takes man out of the universe and the framework of religion and puts him in the middle of events, God remains at the centre of the Spanish play. Calderon's view of human life is above all theocentric. His dramas are not psychological but symbolic. They bring to life for our edification a supernatural order of things. Calderon sees the world as a theatre, in which men play the parts assigned to them by God. This conception is found in Plato and appears again and again in ancient and medieval writers; but "Calderon is the first writer to make the God-directed *theatrum mundi* the subject of a

sacred drama" (E. R. Curtius). Just as the world is a theatre,
so the theatre is also a world: at any rate for Calderon, who
unfolds an amazing wealth of life on the stage. "Calderon's
work as a whole possesses the dimensions of a world-theatre
inasmuch as the characters act their parts against a cosmic
background" (E. R. Curtius).

Everything that happens takes place here within the limits
of a settled order which reflects the consciousness of an age
whose monarchical and Catholic framework had not yet been
shaken. Therefore in Calderon's plays faith, honour, patriotism
and loyalty to the king are the highest moral values. Yet, for
all the stability of the world-order which it portrays, Calderon's
work displays a freedom of form and content unparalleled in
the rest of Europe. For him art is a game played before God,
and so he gains a freedom and innocence which put the earthly
in harmony with the supernatural and adorn even the high
seriousness of the mysteries with gay flourishes. Certainly
ancient and oriental elements contribute to this playful un-
concern—Goethe rightly said: "Only he who knows and loves
Hafis can understand Calderon's art"—but at bottom Calderon's light-heartedness rests on his Catholic attitude to life,
which even in Spain is by no means so gloomy as is sometimes
asserted. Calderon's plays confirm Chesterton's words: "Catholic doctrine may be a wall, but it is the wall of a playground.
Christianity is the only framework that has preserved the joy
of the pagan world. . . . The outer perimeter of Christianity
is a strong barrier of moral prohibitions: but inside this inhuman barrier we find the old human life, with children
dancing and men drinking their wine; for Christianity is the
only framework for pagan freedom."

One of Calderon's most famous plays is the tragedy *The
Steadfast Prince*. Its hero, Don Fernando of Portugal, falls
during a war into the hands of the Moors. He could be freed
if the Christian town of Ceuta were sacrificed as a ransom. But
Fernando's conscience will not let him hand over Christian
churches to unbelievers. Neither promises nor threats can

the king receives a crown and purple robe, Beauty a bouquet of flowers, the rich man gold and silver, Wisdom cowl and scourge, the farmer a spade, and the beggar—nothing. The play which they are to act is called "Do right, for God is God!" Two doors for the entrance and exit of the actors symbolize cradle and grave. God sits as audience on a raised upper stage. The "Law of Grace" speaks the prologue and then acts as prompter. All except Wisdom do not play their parts properly. Beauty cannot get on with Wisdom, the rich man plumes himself on his wealth, the farmer complains of hard work and oppressive taxes, and the king misuses his power. They will not listen to the advice of the Law of Grace. The beggar vainly approaches each of them in turn for alms. Beauty is busy with her own adornment and scarcely looks at the beggar, the rich man rebuffs him, the king sends him to his minister, and the farmer wants him to work. Only Wisdom gives him a piece of bread. When the actors are called away by a voice from the grave, they repent. Only the rich man persists in his attitude. The call does not surprise Wisdom, for it has always longed and prepared for death. The World takes away each actor's insignia again. The judgement follows at God's banquet with the chalice and host: the beggar and Wisdom are lifted up to him at once. Beauty, the king and the farmer must pass through the fire of purgatory before they can enter into heavenly bliss. Only the rich man is shut out for ever. The epilogue, spoken by the World, once again formulates the theme: human life is a drama enacted before the eyes of God.

By their profundity, their visual power and their universality Calderon's plays have aroused the admiration of the greatest critics. It is no wonder that he has remained a source of inspiration for many writers until today. In England, Dryden, Shelley, Bridges and T. S. Eliot were all influenced by him; in France, Claudel recognized his debt to him; and in Germany and Austria, Tieck, Eichendorff, Immerman and Grillparzer in the nineteenth century, and Hugo von Hofmannsthal, Richard von Kralik and Wilhelm von Scholz in the twentieth century all learnt from him.

FRANCE

Francis de Sales (1567–1622)

Leigh Hunt called Francis de Sales "the gentleman saint", and in fact this saintly nobleman from Savoy did prove by his life the truth of the lesson inculcated in his writings: that one can be a highly cultivated man of the world and at the same time completely permeated by the love of God; that a man can live under the conditions of modern civilization without suffering damage to his soul; and that a humanistic education need not weaken piety, but on the contrary can strengthen it and transform it into saintliness. In his teaching, as in his life, Francis de Sales brought to splendid completion what Thomas More, Vittoria Colonna, Ignatius of Loyola and Teresa of Avila had begun in theory and practice: the reconciliation of Christianity and culture.

In his *Sermons*, in his *Letters* and in his books, *Philothea* and *Theotimus*, the Bishop of Geneva was a spiritual adviser of genius. With splendid magnanimity he refused to measure everyone by the same standard. He knew that there are different kinds of piety, that there are many paths to heaven, and that there is more than one means to perfection:

> Piety is found to take different forms; it will not be the same in the highly-placed as in the day-labourer, in the prince as in the subject, in the young girl as in the wife or widow. As well as his position in society, the individual's personal strength, his occupations and his duties will dictate the manner of his godliness. It would be unfitting if a bishop lived like a hermit, if people of noble birth renounced earthly goods like the Capuchins, or if a craftsman wanted to spend the whole day in church.

True piety is possible in any situation, but must always be adapted to it. There are as many kinds of saintliness as there are saints. Intrinsically it was an old Christian doctrine that one can be blessed in any condition. But in the Middle Ages the monastic ideal moved so much into the foreground that the impression was bound to arise that the Christian could only attain perfection in the cloister. Francis emphatically denied this. Holiness is not the prerogative of a few chosen souls who have fled the world; it is the goal prescribed for *all* Christians. If his methods were tolerant, his demands were unyielding. It says unmistakably in the New Testament: "You shall be perfect . . . that is the will of God, your sanctification. . . . Pursue sanctification, without which no one can look upon the Lord!" To fulfil these demands it is not necessary to go into the cloister. Francis de Sales wished to eradicate the prejudice that no man of the world could attain perfection, and to bring holiness into the world. In this, for his age, he is amazingly modern and a real pioneer. The fact that his work *Philothea* (the "Introduction to a Devout Life") was at the time contradicted, attacked and even burnt shows clearly enough how novel his attitude seemed. While the late medieval *Imitation of Christ* was addressed to people in monasteries and convents, Francis de Sales wrote his *Philothea* expressly to instruct "those who live in the bustle of the world, in towns, in the family circle, even at the court—those who are compelled to deal with the people of the world and for this very reason often do not have the courage to think that a devout way of life is possible for them, too". Solitude, one of the most important means to spiritual perfection, is attainable in other places besides the cloister and the wilderness. There is also such a thing as spiritual solitude, into which a man can retire during the greatest activity: "Even if you are in the midst of a crowd you can be alone with your God." Piety in the world, which can at times be more difficult to practise than flight from the world, was the new ideal which Francis proclaimed. Fundamentally it was an old ideal, which at that time had become forgotten and even today has lost none of its validity.

Francis de Sales did not share the view that the religious life consisted in the accomplishment of exceptional works. Ascetic achievements can easily make a man complacent and presumptuous and cause him to forget how dependent his sanctification is on God's grace. Francis advised people to be satisfied with the opportunities and means at their disposal. With the desire for the exceptional he contrasted the homely exercises of everyday life: "Those daily little works of charity, toothache, the unfriendliness and neglect of others, the curious mood of your husband or your wife, a broken glass, a lost glove, the small discomfort of going to bed a little earlier and getting up a little earlier when you have to go to church—all these little burdens should be accepted and borne with love; that pleases God greatly." It is of more service to bear the cross that God has laid upon us against our inclination than the one we have chosen ourselves. Sales put no great value on bodily chastisement. He was not concerned to suppress passions, but to transform them. If human emotions are directed towards lofty goals, they become virtues. Natural needs and strivings are in themselves good, for God put them in men. Even Thomas Aquinas had taught that. With Francis de Sales this ancient Catholic conviction received a fresh accent. He considered it perfectly compatible with piety to dress fashionably, to go to the theatre and to attend balls.

He had no time for the piety that advertises itself by wearing a dismal expression. For him, sadness was not a sign of love of God but its enemy. He wrote to Madame de Chantal, who was inclined to melancholy: "I do not want a special, restless, sad, peevish, bad-tempered sort of piety; it should be mild, gentle, pleasant, peaceful; in a word, free and happy, pleasing to God and man. . . . Awaken often in your heart the feeling of joy and happiness, and firmly believe that this is the true spirit of piety." In this Francis de Sales agrees with Thomas More, Teresa of Avila and Ignatius of Loyola.

All the charm of this religious writer is displayed in the wonderful Letters to St Jeanne Françoise de Chantal. In them we read:

> Above all, holy freedom and magnanimity must prevail. We should have no other law, no other compulsion but that of love. . . . Everything should be done out of love and nothing from compulsion. . . . I leave you the spirit of freedom, not the

freedom which releases us from obedience, for that is the freedom of the flesh, but the freedom which releases us from compulsion, worry and haste. [Francis liked to praise holy calm and indifference!] Why should we care whether we walk through wildernesses or gardens, so long as God is with us. . . . We must suffer others, but first of all ourselves, and we must have patience with our own imperfections.

He often refers to events in the Bible:

St Peter, so Scripture says, was frightened when he saw the violent storm; and as soon as he felt fear he began to sink and drown, and called out: "Lord, save me!" And our Lord took him by the hand and said to him: "O thou of little faith, why hast thou doubted?" Consider this holy apostle: he walks dry-shod on the waters, and the winds and waves do not let him sink; but fear of the wind and waves would have let him sink if the Lord had not held him up. Fear is a greater evil than the evil itself. O daughter of little faith, what do you fear? Have no fear. You walk on the sea amidst the waves, but with Jesus: what is there to fear? But if fear seizes you, then call aloud: "O Lord, save me." He will give you his hand; hold it fast and walk on joyfully. In short, do not philosophize over your evil, make no reply to it, walk on bravely. God will not want to lose you, if, in order not to lose him, you live in accordance with our resolves. And if the world passes away, and everything lies in darkness, smoke and ruins, God is with us. For if God dwells in darkness and on Mount Sinai, amid smoke, thunder, lightning and the raging of the elements, are we not then quite near to him?

Not infrequently, Francis de Sales links his reflections to natural phenomena:

I was pondering recently on what some writers say about kingfishers, those small birds which lay their eggs on the bosom of the sea. They build perfectly round nests so firmly pressed together that the seawater cannot get in; there is just a little opening at the top, through which they can draw in air. They put their little ones inside, so that if the sea surprises them they can float about safely on the waves without the nests filling with water and sinking. The air that enters through the little hole acts as a counter-weight and keeps these little balls, these little boats, so well balanced that they never tip over. O my daughter, how I wish that our hearts could be made in the same way, so firmly pressed together, so well shut up on every side that the storms of the world which smite them could not penetrate them, and that they only had an opening towards heaven, so as to breathe only for our Redeemer. And for whom, dear daughter, should this nest be? For the little chicks of him who made it, for the love of God, for divine and heavenly inclinations. But while the kingfishers are building their nests and their little ones are still too weak to withstand the buffets of the waves, God looks after them and cares for them, and stops the sea carrying them away. In the same way, my daughter, the supreme goodness will protect the nest of our hearts for his holy love against all the attacks of the world, or else he will save us from being attacked. Oh, how I love these birds, which are surrounded by water and live on air alone, which hide in the sea and see only the sky! They swim like fish and sing like birds; what pleases me most is that their anchor is cast upwards and not downwards, to protect them against the waves. O, my sisters and daughters, may Jesus so shape us that, surrounded by the world and the flesh, we may live by the spirit; that amid the vanities of earth we may always look up to heaven; that while we live with men we may praise him with the angels; and that our hopes may be always fixed securely on high, in paradise.

Pascal (1623–62)

When we leave the realm of the lovable Francis de Sales and enter the spiritual world of Pascal, a sharper, keener air meets us. Both writers want to win high-minded men of the world for the religious life; but while Francis uses mildness Pascal displays an unyielding strictness. Francis' writings are for those who already believe and have made up their minds to live according to their faith; Pascal's main work, on the contrary, is addressed to those who do not yet believe, but are dissatisfied in their unbelief and seek a truth to which they can completely surrender themselves. Nietzsche considered that

Pascal, with his combination of fervour, intelligence and command of words, was the first of all Christians. T. S. Eliot has said: "I can think of no Christian writer, not Newman even, more to be commended than Pascal to those who doubt, but who have the mind to conceive and the sensibility to feel, the disorder, the futility, the meaninglessness, the mystery of life and suffering, and who can only find peace through a satisfaction of the whole being."

Compared with that of other philosophers, Pascal's thought is somewhat limited in content. But its few themes are firmly grasped, thoroughly assimilated and informed with a glowing intellectual and emotional fervour. He gives warmth to the most abstract theme with the passion of feeling, and investigates questions of the heart with cool detachment. He is always concerned to know the truth and then to communicate this knowledge convincingly. Hence his eloquence, which, without making use of long words, achieves a direct effect by sheer clarity. His taste for controversy is striking. His thoughts develop from the thoughts of his opponents. To their thesis he opposes his own antithesis. From his passion for argument, which comes out most clearly in the *Lettres provinciales* (Provincial Letters), springs his liking for the dialogue and dialectic.

There is a close connection between Pascal's life and his thought. His development can be divided into three periods. Each of these periods is linked to a stage of existence which is not abandoned at the transition to the next period but retained, although in a new way. In the first period Pascal devoted himself as a mathematician, physicist and engineer almost exclusively to scientific investigation. His ambition made him strive to be a man of learning. In the next period he continued his scientific investigations, but a new dimension was added to his thinking: the realm of wit and culture. Now he studied man and developed into a psychologist and philosopher. His ideal was the *honnête homme*, the cultivated gentleman. In the third and last period Pascal lived entirely for religion. He did not cease to be a scientist and gentleman, but now his highest aim was to become a saint.

This last period began in 1654 with Pascal's conversion, which is recorded in the famous *Memorial*. In this mystic hour Pascal consecrated himself to the living God, who is "not the God of the philosophers", but "the God of Abraham, Isaac and Jacob."

He now produced religious books like the essay *On the Conversion of the Sinner*, the *Sketch of the Life of Jesus*, the reflections on *The Secret of Jesus*, the *Comparison between the Christians of Olden Times and those of Today* and the *Prayer for the Beneficial Use of Illnesses*, which is stylistically one of Pascal's most perfect creations: a masterpiece of rhetorical prose and at the same time a document of deep piety. His conversion did not "break" Pascal, as Nietzsche said it did: his most important mathematical and literary work dates from after 1654. "Pascal showed that one can be both a great, free and independent thinker and a humble Christian who takes seriously every word that comes from Christ and his Church" (Rüttenauer).

Pascal's piety was stamped with the imprint of the convent of Port-Royal, where he spent the last years of his life. Port-Royal was the fortress of Jansenism, whose austere religiosity can be compared with Puritanism. Pascal did not fail to take part in the dispute between Jansenists and Jesuits. He passionately opposed the Society of Jesus, whose moral theologians he reproached with offering Christianity at too cheap a price and meeting human weakness with too many concessions. He published in serial form his *Letters to a Provincial from one of his Friends*, in which he reports on the dispute that has arisen between theologians in Paris, himself playing the part of the unprejudiced observer who seeks information from both sides about the points at issue. He mocks his opponents with irony, malice and wit. The *Provincial Letters* became "the most inspired piece of controversial writing in the literature of the world" (Wasmuth). They are not always fair and just. In the heat of combat Pascal often allowed himself to be carried away into using a violent and caustic tone, and even misrepresentation and distortion.

In the midst of success, after the appearance of the eighteenth letter, Pascal discontinued the series. Perhaps he felt that the dispute was too marginal. Already he could see a greater task before him: a campaign against the educated atheists of his time who despised the Christian religion. A great work was planned, which long illness and an early death prevented him from completing. What remained was a disorderly mass of notes, sketches and fragments—stones for the construction of a defence of Christianity. They appeared after his death as *Pensées sur la religion* (*Thoughts on Religion*). In them Pascal had scaled heights that left the quarrel between Jansenists and Jesuits far below. This fragmentary work made him the greatest Christian thinker and writer of modern times; only Newman can claim the right to stand by his side.

No doubt an inner order, a secret plan lies beneath the *Thoughts*, and what Pascal said of the Bible is also true of the *Thoughts*: "Every author has a meaning in which all contradictions are reconciled. . . . We must therefore seek a meaning which brings into harmony the passages which contradict each other." A key to the understanding of the *Pensées* is provided by Pascal's doctrine of orders of things, whose central importance has already been indicated by Guardini and Wasmuth. They are the three orders to which the three periods of Pascal's life are related. These three realms or dimensions of existence determine the internal construction of his philosophy.

To each of the three realms of existence corresponds a special method or mode of knowledge. For the natural order, only the mathematical or experimental method, the "esprit de géometrie" is suitable. Like his contemporaries, Pascal considers the mathematical method the most perfect of all methods; but at the same time he is conscious of its limits. With it only a certain number of subjects can be mastered. The scientist is easily led by the perfection of his method to overestimate its value in the comprehension of reality as a whole. Pascal was far from imagining that the fullness of the world could be grasped geometrically.

Knowledge of things in the spiritual order, especially the knowledge of men, is reserved to another mode of knowledge, the "esprit de finesse". It comprehends with one glance what the mathematician would grope for in vain. Here the truth is no longer recognized by the senses and the intelligence, through observation and thought, but by feeling, by intuition, by an inner vision. Pascal was combating two opposing currents of thought. The rationalists, convinced of the reliability of rational knowledge, fail to see that in the orders beyond its ken reason can accomplish nothing. The sceptics, who from these limitations of reason deduce that all human knowledge must be limited, fail to see that reason is not the only mode of knowledge. Thus both sides fall into error.

The third and highest order is the supernatural order. It is infinitely superior to the spiritual order, just as the spiritual order is itself infinitely superior to the natural order. As the knowledge of spiritual things infinitely surpasses the knowledge of natural things, it follows that the knowledge of supernatural things must be infinitely superior to the knowledge of spiritual things. Supernatural things are neither grasped by reason nor felt by intuition; they are rather simultaneously grasped and felt in faith and bestowed by grace. Faith thus outstrips reason and feeling without superseding them. One must doubt where necessary, and one must submit where necessary. Some people break these rules "by doubting everything because they do not know that one must submit, or by submitting in everything because they do not know when one should use one's judgement. True Christianity consists of submission *and* the use of reason."

Experience shows that although the three orders and the three modes of knowledge are complementary and can blend harmoniously they by no means form an obvious unity in real life. Body and mind are in constant opposition to each other, man feels unhappy and longs for a harmony that he only knows in theory. Everything seems to indicate that human nature is corrupt and has fallen from its original heights.

Taking these facts of experience as his premises, Pascal unfolds the Christian view of man.

Man is a riddle to himself and "the most wonderful object in nature. For he cannot understand what the body is, still less what the mind is, and least of all how a body can be linked to a mind. That is the climax of his difficulty, and precisely in that lies his real nature." For it is the nature of man to unite in himself two orders of existence, infinitely far apart from each other. Mathematical infinity is only a symbol of this infinity in us. For between our physical nature and our spiritual nature there yawns an abyss as infinite as that between the finite and the infinite. Infinite, too, is the abyss which divides us from the supernatural order, from God; but in spite of this we are *capax Dei*, capable of sharing in God.

Pascal's philosophizing on man is governed by the dialectical method. He only considers it possible to analyse man's contradictory and enigmatic nature by means of thesis and antithesis. The dialectical method is also justified by the fact that human perception is limited in perspective and can only see one side of a thing at a time. That is why Pascal says: "At the end of every truth one must add that one remembers the opposite truth. If there is ever a time when one must recognize two exactly opposite truths, and objections are raised, then leave one of them out." For this reason Pascal's utterances on the nature of man are full of paradoxes and antitheses: "Man is by nature believing and unbelieving; timid and bold. . . . What a chimaera man is! What a curiosity, what a monster, what a chaos, what a mass of contradictions, what a marvel! Judge of all things, miserable worm; master of the truth, sewer of error; glory and dregs of the universe." And of all the contrasts which go to make up man the greatest is the contrast between his greatness and his misery.

"Man's greatness lies in his ability to think." The universe embraces man in its extent and swallows him up like a pinpoint, but through thought man embraces the universe. The universe knows nothing of its own greatness; but man is aware of his weakness. Therein lies his superiority to the universe. "Man is only a reed, the weakest in nature; but he is a thinking reed." In the capacity to think, that is, in reason, lies man's dignity.

But reason is imperfect and limited; therein lies man's misery. Reason and the senses are continually at war with each other and deceive each other; this is the biggest cause of human errors. Man cannot know perfectly either things or himself. Man is also miserable through his passions. A continual struggle rages between reason and the passions. This war "has brought it about that those who want peace are divided into two parties. One party has renounced the passions, and its members want to become gods; the others have renounced reason and want to become animals. But neither party has succeeded in finding peace in this way. Reason is still there to criticize the baseness and injustice of the passions . . . and the passions are still alive in those who wish to renounce them." So man cannot attain peace. It would be pleasant "if there were only reason without passions; or only passions without reason. But as both exist, man cannot live without struggling, for he can only be at peace with one if he is struggling with the other. So he is always divided and in contradiction with himself."

"All this misery proves his greatness. It is the misery of a dethroned king. . . . For who considers himself unhappy because he is not king except a dethroned king? Man's greatness is so evident that it can even be deduced from his misery, for what is natural in animals"—limitation of knowledge, enslavement to instinct, sorrow and death—"we call misery in man."

Since today his nature is like that of the animals, we can see that he has fallen from a better nature which was once his own. . . . If man had never been corrupted, in his innocence he would confidently enjoy truth and bliss; and if man had never been anything but corrupt he would have no conception of truth or bliss. . . . We have a conception of happiness and cannot attain it; we have a dim picture of truth and possess only false-hood. . . . So clear is it that we were once on a plane of perfection from which we have unhappily plunged down. [Man is] obviously confused, has fallen from his true position and cannot find it again. He seeks it everywhere, in impenetrable darkness, full of disquiet and without success.

Man wants to be happy. But how is he to go about it? He would have to make himself immortal. As this is impossible and he can find no cure for uncertainty, sorrow and death, he turns his thoughts away from these things and takes refuge in entertainment. But this gives rise to fresh unhappiness: restlessness, fear of boredom, and disgust.

It is dangerous to remind man too much of his likeness to animals without showing him his greatness. It is also dangerous to let him feel his greatness too much without showing him his baseness. It is still more dangerous to leave him in ignorance about both. But it is very profitable to draw his attention to both. "Man is neither angel nor animal, and the misfortune is that anyone who tries to make him an angel makes him into an animal."

What is man to do after he has recognized his greatness as well as his baseness?

He should love himself, for there is a nature capable of good in him; but he should not on that account love the baseness that is in him. He should despise himself; for this capacity is powerless; but he should not on that account despise this capacity. He should hate himself and also love himself. . . . All these contradictions, which seemed to remove me furthest from the knowledge of religion, have in fact led me most swiftly to the true religion. . . . The true religion would have to teach man his greatness and his misery; it would have to bring him to respect himself and despise himself, hate himself and love himself.

It would have to have recognized the true nature of man. "Who has recognized it except Christianity?"

Only the Christian religion solves the riddle of man. It

teaches him that his greatness springs from his likeness to God, and his misery from his fall from God; that man's longing for happiness and his inability to attain happiness testify that he once possessed happiness, but lost it; that this lost happiness left behind a gap which man tries to fill with everything possible, but only God can fill; and that man needs grace in order to be reunited with God. Thus Christianity shows man his true condition, the reasons for it, and the means by which he can be healed.

What have men managed to do without this divine knowledge? Some have regarded nature as uncorrupted, others as irreparably damaged, and they have been unable to escape either the pride or the indolence which are the two sources of all vices. For if they recognized the perfection of man, they would know nothing of his corruption; then they would avoid indolence, but lose themselves in pride. And if they recognized the weakness of nature, they would know nothing of its dignity; then they could avoid vanity, but only by plunging into despair. Only the Christian religion has been able to cure these two vices [pride and despair]. . . . For it reveals to the just, whom it elevates to participation in divinity itself, that even in this sublime condition they carry in themselves the source of all corruption, which makes them throughout their lives subject to error, misery, death and sin; and it reminds the most abandoned that they are capable of receiving the grace of their Redeemer. By thus giving cause for trembling to those whom it justifies and comfort to those whom it condemns, in its great justice it tempers fear with hope, by means of this double capacity, common to all, for grace and sin. Thus it humbles man far more than reason alone could, but without casting him into despair, and raises him far higher than pride raises nature, but without making him conceited. By this it makes clear that only the Christian religion, which alone is without error and vice, can teach and improve man. . . . Therefore it teaches men at the same time these two truths: that there is a God, whom men can attain, and that in nature there is a corruption which makes them unworthy of him. It is equally important for man to recognize both these truths; it is equally dangerous for him to know God without knowing his own wretchedness, and to know his own wretchedness without knowing the Redeemer who can cure him of it.

"If man knows God without knowing his own wretchedness, he falls a victim to pride. If he knows his own wretchedness without knowing God, he falls a prey to despair. Through the knowledge of Jesus Christ we stand in the middle, for in it we find God as well as our own wretchedness." Thus Pascal's philosophy reaches its climax in the worship of God-made-man, without whom the world would not endure and man could not know God. "Jesus Christ is the goal of everything and the centre towards which everything strives. He who knows him knows the ground of all things."

Racine (1637–99)

When Pascal was living the last days of his life at Port-Royal he must have seen among the pupils of the convent school the young Racine. Racine's Jansenist upbringing invites a comparison with Corneille, who grew up in the opposite camp. And in fact the two dramatists of the classical age have often been contrasted with each other on a Jansenist-Jesuit basis. Thus a liberal historian of ideas, Fülöp-Miller, writes:

> Corneille was educated at the Jesuit Collège de Clermont, and his dramas were to bring Molinism on to the stage. His characters work out their own fate; they are unaware of original sin, they believe in the freedom of their decisions, and know how to overcome even the strongest passions by the exercise of will-power. On the other hand, the tragedies of Racine, who was brought up in the atmosphere of Port-Royal, are a dramatic formulation of the Jansenist doctrine that men are helpless victims of their passions unless God illumines and saves them through his grace. . . . The tragic end of Racine's characters is always intended to impress on the audience the inescapability of the fate imposed by God.

The individual details of this comparison may be somewhat exaggerated in order to sharpen the contrast, but on the whole it is a just one. Corneille's plays are all action, while in Racine's there is little outward action; the real action takes place inside the human soul. Strictness of form, sublimity of gesture and speech, the pomp and rhythm of the verse are common to both poets; but Racine's style is more intimate, more reserved, more expressive than Corneille's. It springs from a different attitude to the world and therefore has a different effect. Corneille's play *Polyeucte*, in which Roman heroism is defeated by the Christian spirit of martyrdom, confirms Goethe's saying that Corneille exerts an effect capable of making heroes. In contrast Racine's tragedies, with their sublime pathos of renunciation, will stir no one to heroic deeds, but in their quiet, penetrating way they may well bring home to noble souls the value of suffering and sacrifice.

The wonderfully musical verse of this most French of all writers has only been fully appreciated in France itself, where it still exerts considerable influence, as François Mauriac's plays show. Since in the last analysis poetry is untranslatable, outside his own country Racine has not been appreciated at his true worth, and even Schiller's translation of *Phèdre* did not succeed in winning him a lasting position on the German stage. Lessing's attacks on the French classical drama built up a certain prejudice which, in spite of Vossler's and R. A. Schröder's efforts, has not yet been overcome. This distaste may be limited purely to the form of Racine's plays, but the result is that a great religious poet of the West is hardly given a hearing in Germany. Much the same is true of England, where Racine is only played occasionally, and then in French by visiting companies from Paris.

Racine tried to be at the same time a good Christian and a skilful courtier. For some time he kept aloof from the Jansenists, but his *Sketch of the History of Port-Royal* shows the warmth of the religious ties by which he was bound. "The historiographer, panegyrist and enthusiastic admirer of his king felt just as much in the right and bound by duty as the Christian" (R. A. Schröder). Occasionally he did find the tension unbearable. In one of his *Spiritual Songs* we find these lines:

> O God, what cruel strife!
> Two men quarrel in my breast.
> One wishes with all his heart
> Always to be obedient to you,
> The other wishes to lead me astray
> With rebellions and sinful desires.

These lines are written round a passage in the Epistle to the Romans, but almost certainly also express a personal experience.

Racine's tragedies remind us of Euripides. But his characters differ from the heroes of ancient tragedy in heart and conscience. Racine shifts the tragic conflict into the loneliness of the individual conscience. He is the founder and classical practitioner of the modern psychological drama. All his conflicts are seen from the Christian angle, even if they are set in an antique frame. In *Phèdre*, for example, the terrible old legend is humanized, and even the love-tragedies *Andromaque* and *Bérénice* are no less Christian in conception than the two biblical dramas *Esther* and *Athalie*. Antiquity and Christianity are intimately linked together in these plays, but Christianity is the dominant partner.

Racine's biblical dramas, *Esther* and *Athalie*, are works of a special kind which differ in every respect from his other plays. They were not intended for the stage, but for the young ladies of the aristocratic girls' school at Saint-Cyr, and therefore have an edifying, courtly and humanistic tone. The choruses give them a lyrical movement. In *Esther* the horrors of the biblical subject are toned down or concealed, and there are even touches of humour.

Athalie, on the other hand, is filled with the spirit of prophecy; it is not mild and sweet in tone like *Esther*, but mysterious, frightening and sublime. In a tiny space and with the most fragile instruments God here executes a judgement that determines the course of earthly events for thousands of years. The actors in the drama appear as the vessels, victims and agents of a higher dispensation. *Athalie* is "a historical drama of politics and religion, in which king and God, royal families and priestly dynasties struggle against each other. . . . Confusion and consternation lie over the whole action, whose meaning those concerned only divine and do not clearly see. For 'history belongs to God', and what happens in *Athalie* is a prelude to the most overwhelming events in the history of mankind. It is the mighty birth-pangs of Christianity bursting-out of the old Covenant" (Vossler). One of the key passages is Joad's speech to the young king:

"You have not yet felt the intoxication of royal power, nor heard the flatterer's seductive words: laws, even holy ones, are only valid for the people; they leave the prince free. He is bound only by his own will. No sacrifice is too great for his fame. Kings are allowed to wield an iron sceptre; the common herd is condemned to toil and tears."

Such foolish words led to destruction. Even the king is subject to the law. The high priest reminds the king of this again at the end of the play: "Know, King of the Jews, and never forget, that kings have a stern judge in heaven, innocence an avenger, and orphans a father." With these words, which the Sun-king, Louis XIV, was at liberty to apply to himself, Racine concludes his masterpiece; and with them he takes his leave for ever of the stage. He renounced the theatre completely. In the last decade of his life he wrote nothing but the *Spiritual Songs*, austere, matter-of-fact paraphrases of biblical texts, adaptations of hymns from the Roman breviary, and the *Sketch of the History of Port-Royal*, "the greatest historical work of the seventeenth century" (Lanson).

Bossuet (1627–1704)

We find it distasteful that almost all the great men of France in the age of Louis XIV paid court to a king who was not guided by Christian principles in his personal life, in his politics, in his relations with the Catholic Church or in his attitude to the Protestants and Jansenists. We have already made the acquaintance of one panegyrist of Louis in the person of Racine. He is far surpassed in this respect by Bossuet, the Bishop of Meaux. This brilliant man, one of the greatest masters of French prose, put his learning and his eloquence almost completely at the service of the king and became Louis' most typical mouthpiece. No one has glorified more emphatically the system of absolute monarchy, no one has praised in more decisive terms the alliance of throne and altar, no one did battle more energetically for the so-called freedom of the Gallican Church than Bossuet. But much as we may deplore the fateful part played by the Bishop of Meaux in political history, we cannot deny him an eminent position in the history of Christian literature.

For the Dauphin, whose tutor he was, Bossuet wrote the *Treatise on the Knowledge of God and of Oneself* and the *Outline of Universal History*. Both books were long used in French schools. In his *Outline of Universal History* Bossuet develops his philosophy of history. For him the course of world events is the story of the rise of God's kingdom. The pre-Christian peoples prepare the ground for the foundation and development of the Christian Church. The driving force in history is divine providence. Its intervention "causes kingdoms to pass away, and thrones to tumble amid dreadful tumult, so that we may feel that there is no firm ground beneath men's feet, and that impermanence and disquiet are the inescapable lot of humanity".

As a preacher of classical sermons, Bossuet is one of the greatest phenomena of all ages. Individual passages in his *Panegyric of St Paul* are among the finest productions of Christian eloquence. His six *Funeral Orations*, delivered on the occasion of the death of eminent persons, are among the most perfect things of their kind that French literature can show, and it is not poor in masterpieces of oratory. They are distinguished by sublimity of thought, depth of feeling and purity of taste. These solemn funeral orations are the only sermons that Bossuet prepared completely beforehand. All his other *Sermons* he delivered without preparation after a short meditation. Those which have come down to us were written down by people who heard them.

Bossuet's sermons draw on all the wealth of biblical phraseology and imagery. They usually deal with moral themes, and condemn vices more often than they praise virtues. They pillory above all ambition, selfishness, covetousness, intemperance and injustice. In the presence of the king Bossuet declared that the source of these vices was pride and "the intoxication of great power, which is so fruitful in crimes, and produces men like Nero and Nebuchadnezzar". He used to speak boldly and freely, and although his friend Arnauld said of him that he had never had the courage to remonstrate with the king, this does not seem to be in character. Bossuet certainly lacked apostolic frankness in many situations. He spoke selfconsciously to his listeners: "My sermon, which you think to judge, will judge you on the Last Day, and if you do not leave here as better Christians, then you leave laden with all the more guilt."

Bossuet achieved his greatest success during his lifetime with his numerous writings in defence of the Catholic faith against reformers. His brilliantly written *Explanation of Catholic Doctrine on Controversial Points* was intended less to demonstrate the truth of Catholic doctrine than to portray it in its true form and free from the distortions which traditional Protestant attacks had fastened on to it. This book, which consists of only sixty pages, is simple and unpretentious in style, and refrains from making any attacks on Protestant doctrine. Its impact was tremendous: it was translated into German, English, Dutch, Italian and Latin; in France, Germany and England a flood of rejoinders appeared; the pope and numerous bishops gave their solemn approval to Bossuet's work; and many leading Protestants, including Marshal Turenne, were converted to Catholicism after reading it.

The *History of the Differences between the Protestant Churches*, a masterpiece of clear and eloquent exposition, tries to demonstrate the falseness of Protestantism by a consideration of the variations in its creeds and teaching. In basic intention this book is irenic. Its aim is to illuminate the obscurity in which passion and misunderstanding had veiled ecclesiastical controversy. It seeks to play down rather than emphasize the doctrinal differences between Protestantism and Catholicism and brings to the forefront those aspects of Protestant creeds and theology which show an apparent or real approximation to the teaching of the Church. Bossuet made a serious effort, as his *Correspondence with Leibniz* shows, to effect a reunion of the separated Churches. It is regrettable that the repeal of the Edict of Nantes, which has rightly been regarded as one of the greatest blots on the history of France, was openly praised by Bossuet in his Funeral Oration for the Chancellor Le Tellier.

In spite of all his weaknesses the "Eagle of Meaux" achieved a fame that has lasted until today. It is true that today Bossuet's reputation rests more on the brilliance of his style than on the content of his works. His political and ecclesiastical views are now shared by scarcely anyone. Nevertheless in the nineteenth and twentieth centuries important figures like F. Brunetière, Charles Maurras and Paul Claudel have acknowledged their adherence to principles of Bossuet's.

Fénelon (1651–1715)

One of the most important of the doctrinal disputes in which Bossuet played a leading part was the quarrel over Quietism. Quietism demanded complete unselfishness in man's love for God and complete passivity in his surrender to God. This doctrine, preached by Mme de Guyon, was opposed by Bossuet but warmly defended by Fénelon. So the Bishop of Meaux and the Archbishop of Cambrai came into conflict. After they had exchanged a number of pamphlets, Bossuet succeeded in having Fénelon's *Explanation of the Principles of the Saints on the Spiritual Life* condemned by the pope. In the dispute with Fénelon Bossuet displayed the least attractive side of his character. From the point of view of dogma he won the day, but Fénelon was the moral victor. His declaration of submission ends with the words: "God forbid that we should ever be mentioned except as a shepherd who recognized that it was his duty to show more obedience than the last sheep in the flock."

Like Bossuet, Fénelon also acted as a royal tutor, but with incomparably greater success. For his pupil, Louis XIV's eldest grandson, he wrote the didactic novel *The Adventures of Telemachus,* whose classical style and lively characterization made it an extremely influential book. Telemachus, the son of Odysseus, is taught by his tutor Mentor, and by his own experience, that virtue brings happiness and vice unhappiness, and that one must therefore always tread "the straight path and unchanging way" of virtue, and let impulse be governed by reason. The universally binding command of virtue knows no distinctions of rank, and God makes his demands even on the ruler. The novel thus becomes a royal mirror, which is to show the future king from examples how the ruler should behave and how he should not. The principle that the prince must live and work for his people, the assertion that his power is limited by the laws, the demand that he should not interfere in religious questions, the wish for a peaceful policy, the rejection of imperialism and wars of conquest, the criticism of luxury, the warning against flatterers and the condemnation of inordinate ambition, which is particularly heavily punished in hell, were all felt by Louis XIV as criticisms of his own régime. The angry king banned the book.

Fénelon also displayed exceptional frankness towards the king on another occasion. He wrote a bold *Letter* to Louis XIV which makes clear how different Fénelon's opinion of absolutism was from Bossuet's:

Sire, the person who takes it upon himself to address this letter to you has absolutely no interest in this world that might guide your hand. . . . With all your power, there is nothing you could give him that he would desire; and he would gladly suffer all the ills of the world to bring home to you those truths without which no king can be great and good. . . . Your tutors have taught you no other art of governing than one composed of mistrust, jealousy, complete absence of virtue, fear of any meritorious act, a taste for submissive, cringing people, arrogance of attitude and behaviour, and a preference for anything that makes you great and glorious. For thirty years your ministers have first shaken and then overturned all the pillars of the constitution in order to make the king's power as absolute as possible. The whole language of the court has changed; one hears no more of the state and the constitution, but only of the king and the king's will. . . . You have been lauded to the skies, because you unite all greatness in your own person alone, that is, you have made all France poor. In order to introduce a dangerous and injurious luxury at your court, the ruler's friends have tried to raise the court on the ruins of every class in the kingdom, as if you could become great by making your subjects small, whereas the greatness of a kingdom's subjects is the true foundation of all royal greatness. . . . Local governors have accustomed the royal ear to hearing continually nothing but exaggerated praise, praise which went to the point of deification and which you ought to have contemptuously rejected for the sake of your own salvation. The royal name has been made hateful and the French nation has been made intolerable to its neighbours. It could find no lasting ally because it only wanted slaves. Bloody wars have been started, for example in 1672 against Holland. I have purposely mentioned this war in particular because it was the source of all the others, and because it had no other motive but the desire for fame and revenge, a motive that can never stamp a war with the seal of justice. It follows that all extensions of our frontiers which are a legacy of this war must be regarded as unjust conquests. I know perfectly well that the peace terms obtained seem to conceal the injustice of the conquest because they handed over to you the places captured. But a war that is unjust to start with can never become just by virtue of a successful outcome. The terms which the defeated country signs are not signed freely and willingly. It signs with a knife at its throat simply to avoid still greater losses. It signs like someone handing over his purse in response to the threat "Your money or your life!" So in order to see your conquests as God sees them you must go back to the origin of the Dutch war. It is useless to say that the conquests you have made were necessary to your state. What belongs to someone else can never be necessary to me. Only one thing is really necessary, and that is to act justly. . . . This may suffice to make you realize that your whole career outstepped the bounds of justice and truth, and therefore those of the Gospel. All the terrible events that shook Europe for more than twenty years, all the blood shed like water, all the cruelties practised, all the provinces laid waste, all the towns and villages reduced to ashes were no more than the unhappy results of that unhappy war of 1672, which you started simply out of the desire for glory. . . . Such wanton behaviour united the whole of Europe against you. . . . Alas, Sire, you run the risk of being feared as a cruel master even in your own realm. . . . Your victories and your conquests are no longer a cause for celebration among your people. Full of bitterness and despair, they cannot rejoice with you; on the contrary, the spark of rebellion is gradually kindling in all parts of the country, and the terrible belief is spreading that the king feels no pity for the people's misery and loves only his own power and glory. . . . Sire, that is the state you are in now. And you do not see this state, for you live like one whose eyes are always covered. But God will yet lift the veil from your eyes and show you plainly the things which you would prefer not to see. The sword of justice has long been hanging over your head, the blow is only delayed because the judge is also a father. . . . The Lord will know how to separate his just cause from yours, which is not just. He will know how to humble you, in order to hasten your return to him. For you will never be a Christian, unless you humble yourself before God. . . . You love nothing but your own fame and comfort. You see everything in relation to yourself, as if you were God and everything else only created to do homage to you. Yet the truth is just the reverse: you were put on earth by God only for the good of the people! France is in its last agony. Will those you depend on refrain from telling you the truth until all is lost? What good are these friends of yours if they do not make you understand that you must give back the lands that do not belong to you, make good the wrongs that the Church has suffered at your hands, and direct all your attention to becoming a true Christian before death overtakes you. I know that those who speak this language of Christian freedom run the risk of losing the king's favour; but should the favour of kings be dearer to us than the true well-being of kings? King! You must humble yourself under the mighty hand of God, unless you wish to wait until he humbles you. King! You must first yourself desire peace. and by this self-abasement do penance for all the glory that you have made your idol. King! To save the state, you must give back to our enemies all your conquests which otherwise you can never keep except unjustly. Sire! The person who tells you these truths is so little opposed to the king's highest interests that he would gladly sacrifice his life to see you as God would have you, and he will never, never cease to pray for you.

In his heartfelt and simple *Sermons*, too, Fénelon displayed "the courage to speak the truth in all circumstances and the ability to express it modestly and nobly" (M. Claudius). Fénelon himself fulfilled in practice the demands he made of the bishop. His *Spiritual Letters,* with all their priestly and episcopal warnings, advice and instruction, are permeated by such mild and touching tenderness and friendliness that one can understand the unbounded respect and love which met him on every side. To the Duke of Burgundy he wrote: "Religion does not consist in the anxious observance of petty formalities, but in the virtues proper to the condition of each individual." And to a friend he wrote: "We do more for the truth by edification than by wrangling. It is better to pray for the erring than to confute them." Fénelon used to say that there was no need to prove and defend religion, but only to describe it simply and clearly, for it proved and defended itself. He held the view that actions speak louder than words. For this reason he laid particular emphasis on the value of Church history in education. His book *On the Education of Girls* shows him as an educator of genius. The book is unsurpassed in Christian educational literature. Classical in style and language, it contains a wealth of simple Christian rules of life and principles of education. Fénelon's religious writings were translated into German during his lifetime and exerted considerable influence on Pietism.

Bourdaloue (1632–1704)

The greatest preacher in seventeenth-century France after Bossuet and Fénelon was the Jesuit Louis de Bourdaloue. His contemporaries called him the orator of kings and the king of orators. He lacks Fénelon's depth of feeling and Bossuet's wealth of language, but in the place of rhetorical swing he displays the light, rational elegance of the dawning age of reason. Voltaire rightly says of him: "He is the first to give expression to an always elegant reason."

Bourdaloue despises a pretentious style, baroque pomp and the attempt to play on the emotions, for he wishes neither to move nor to overwhelm, but to convince. He therefore loves above all clarity of exposition and puts his trust solely in the logical force of his arguments. Literary history praises him as the reformer of the French sermon, and the history of Christian piety as a holy and sensible man who was respected even by opponents of the Jesuits.

ENGLAND

Donne (1573–1631)

The baroque age is an age of contrasts. Above all, pleasure in the world and longing for heaven, thirst for knowledge and fervour of faith were carried reciprocally to the highest point, so that in no other age has there been such a passionate striving for harmony. We have already met different variations of this striving in Francis de Sales, Pascal and Racine. The struggle for harmony appears in a still more acute form in some English baroque poets. Of these writers it was John Donne who gave the religious poetry of the time its characteristic stamp.

He was a pioneer in his liking for the abstractions of contemporary philosophy and natural science. He made use of them to express his innermost spiritual life: feelings were transformed into concepts, and concepts into concrete pictures. The "conceit", the connection of things naturally far apart, was long regarded, together with rhetorical force and dialectical acuteness, as the leading characteristic of Donne and his disciples. But Dr Johnson did wrong to look down contemptuously on these "Metaphysicals". What this school created was more than clever intellectual poetry. De Quincey was nearer the truth when he said that few writers had shown a greater compass than Donne, for he had united what no one else had ever united: the sharpest logic with the most powerful imagery. It was precisely this spiritual tension that moved T. S. Eliot to lay such emphasis on Donne; and other poets of today, too, feel drawn by the remarkably divided attitude to life which makes this baroque poet seem so modern.

The self-confidence of Renaissance man had changed by the beginning of the seventeenth century into a feeling of powerlessness forcefully expressed by Donne:

> And new Philosophy calls all in doubt,
> The Element of fire is quite put out;
> The Sun is lost, and th' earth, and no man's wit
> Can well direct him where to looke for it.
> And freely men confesse that this world's spent,
> When in the Planets, and the Firmament
> They seeke so many new; they see that this
> Is crumbled out againe to his Atomies.
>
> (*An Anatomy of the World*, lines 205–212)

Astronomy had torn aside the curtain from the expanses of the universe, and Donne, like Pascal, shuddered at the view. And, again like Pascal, he finally took refuge in the arms of the living God. Shaken by the ignorance of knowledge, the inadequacy of man and the relative worthlessness of this life, the author of the *Anatomy of the World* longed for truth and perfection in God.

He did not immediately gain peace. His whole life long Donne continued to struggle, torn between extremes. He belonged to various different intellectual worlds. He not only studied deeply medieval scholasticism, but also plunged enthusiastically into modern science. His thirst for knowledge of all sorts gave him no rest, and his hunger for intensive experience, both sensual and spiritual, was never satisfied. His poems are, as it were, the deposit of this restless life. We see him entangled in erotic adventures. We find him on Essex's expedition to the Azores and in the fight at Cadiz. We find the scholar bent over folios of theology and the ambitious courtier walking behind great lords and ladies. Brought up a Catholic, Donne later became an agnostic, and finally meets us as an Anglican priest. The erstwhile hedonist wears a hair shirt. The singer of physical passion writes *Divine Poems* and *Holy Sonnets*.

> Oh, to vex me, contraryes meet in one:
> Inconstancy unnaturally hath begott
> A constant habit; that when I would not
> I change in vowes, and in devotione.
> As humorous is my contritione
> As my prophane Love, and as soone forgott:
> As ridlingly distemper'd, cold and hott,
> As praying, as mute; as infinite, as none.
> I durst not view heaven yesterday; and to-day
> In prayers, and flattering speaches I court God:
> Tomorrow I quake with true fears of his rod.
> So my devout fitts come and go away
> Like a fantastique Ague: save that here
> Those are my best dayes, when I shake with feare.

(Holy Sonnets, XIX)

Like Pascal, Donne is moved by the "Riddle" of man, who is a "mixture of contraryes" and seems to have "two souls"; like Pascal, Donne sees man as a microcosm, sharing at the same time in the physical and the spiritual world; and, like Pascal again, Donne can only express this experience in sharp

antitheses and surprising paradoxes; the only difference is that
Pascal uses the language of the philosopher and Donne that
of the lyric poet. In what mighty eruptions the shaken heart
here unloads itself! Water and fire as symbols of destructive
and prodigal powers are ancient images, but Donne makes
them seem new:

> I am a little world made cunningly
> Of Elements, and an Angelike spright,
> But black sinne hath betraid to endlesse night
> · My worlds both parts, and (oh) both parts must die.
> You which beyond that heaven which was most high
> Have found new sphears, and of new lands can write,
> Poure new seas in mine eyes, that so I might
> Drowne my world with my weeping ernestly,
> Or wash it, if it must be drown'd no more:
> But oh it must be burnt! alas the fire
> Of lust and envie have burnt it heretofore,
> And made it fouler; let their flares retire,
> And burne me o Lord, with a fiery zeale
> Of thee and thy house, which doth in eating heale.
>
> (*Holy Sonnets*, V)

Donne's later work lives on a tension so strong that it can
only be broken by volcanic outbursts. The continually unsuccessful attempts to reconcile love of God and love of the
world, the repeated defeats in the struggle to harmonize the
instinctual and spiritual forces in him, remorse, sharpened by
misfortune and illness, and the longing for holiness produce
verses of a heartfelt fervour that strives for total sacrifice of
self. Baroque strings of words, provocative paradoxes and the
hammer-blows of an irregular rhythm are well suited to the
expression of such passionate feelings. The poet is not satisfied
with images of military and political power as symbols of
force; he heightens them into the elemental:

> Batter my heart, three person'd God; for, you
> As yet but knocke, breathe, shine, and seeke to mend;
> That I may rise, and stand, o'erthrow mee', and bend

Your force, to break, blowe, burn and make me new.
I, like an usurpt towne, to' another due,
Labour to' admit you, but Oh, to no end,
Reason your viceroy in mee, mee should defend,
But is captiv'd, and proves weak or untrue.
Yet dearly' I love you', and would be loved faine,
But am betroth'd unto your enemie:
Divorce mee, 'untie, or breake that knot againe,
Take mee to you, imprison mee, for I
Except you enthrall mee, never shall be free,
Nor ever chast, except you ravish mee.

(*Holy Sonnets*, XIV)

In the *Sermons*, which he preached in London as Dean of
St Paul's, Donne had often shaken his audience by painting
the horrors of death. When he himself became acquainted
with them he turned in his sickness and torment to God:

Thou hast made me, and shall thy worke decay?
Repaire me now, for now mine end doth haste,
I runne to death, and death meets me as fast,
And all my pleasures are like yesterday;
I dare not move my dimme eyes any way,
Despaire behind, and death before doth cast
Such terrour, and my feeble flesh doth waste
By sinne in it, which it t'wards hell doth weigh;
Only thou art above, and when towards thee
By thy leave I can looke, I rise againe;
But our old subtle foe so tempteth me,
That not one houre my selfe I can sustaine;
Thy Grace may wing me to prevent his art,
And thou like Adamant draw mine iron heart.

(*Holy Sonnets*, I)

The last comparison sounds original, but occurs 300 years
earlier in the revelations of Bridget of Sweden, where we find:
"Just as the magnet draws iron to itself, so do I, God, draw
hard hearts to me." Thus Donne took much of his imagery
from tradition, but what he expresses in it are the personal
tortures of a man worried about the fate of his immortal soul
and concerned about his relationship to God.

Crashaw (1613–49)

Most English poets of the seventeenth century devoted themselves exclusively either to worldly or to spiritual poetry. But hardly one of them was able to keep heaven and earth completely separate. In the worldly poets the heaven they have denied occasionally descends to earth, and in the religious poets the earth they have excluded steals into heaven. In their verses they preach flight from the world and contempt for earthly goods; but when they compare the deceitful and transitory joys of this life with the true and eternal bliss of heaven they make use of earthly glory and beauty in order to bring to life the splendour of the next world. For Herbert and Vaughan, heaven is "God's fertile garden" or a "magnificent palace", in which all human longings are to be fulfilled. Nature seems to them a revelation of divinity, and so they borrow from it the material for a symbolism that at times certainly seems artificial. In Richard Crashaw's poetry this spiritualized sensuousness, or sensualized spirituality, is raised to an art of lofty beauty which set an example for Milton, Pope, Coleridge and Francis Thompson. As a student at Cambridge, Crashaw made the acquaintance of Spanish mysticism, and St Teresa of Avila became his ideal. He wrote hymns to her when he was still a Protestant, and through her he was converted to Catholicism. Through her, too, he learnt that "love is eloquence," and her books stimulated him to sing in English what they told in Spanish. So the Spanish Teresa gave England a religious poet whose lofty inspiration, unparalleled imagination, ecstatic fervour and colourful style made him the greatest of his age.

Besides a volume of secular lyrics called *The Delights of the Muses*, Crashaw published two volumes of religious poetry, *The Book of Spiritual Epigrams* and *Steps to the Temple*. They contain poems and epigrams based on episodes in the Gospel and sayings of Jesus, reflections on the wounds of the crucified Lord and the tears of Mary, paraphrases of psalms, splendid imitations of liturgical hymns and prayers, and the hymns to the name of Jesus, for Christmas, for New Year, for the Epiphany, for the Assumption, to Mary Magdalen and St Teresa.

A prominent characteristic of Crashaw is his fervour and warmth. He loves "sweetness so sad, sadness so sweet." Tears flow on almost every page: tears of emotion, of repentance, of sorrow and of joy. Such superabundance of feeling is no longer to our taste, and we have to smile when Crashaw asserts that he will "shed thrice three tears to show how genuine his sorrow is." Tears are an essential part of his poetry. But it is impossible to deny that his enthusiasm is genuine, and the fervour of his hymns is based on the reality without which no work of art can be beautiful. It is not permissible for religious poetry to revel in emotion alone, or to divorce emotions from their object and to make them independent. Nor does this occur in Crashaw's poetry. However lively his reactions may be, they are all centred round the objective fact of the divine mystery.

The means which Crashaw employs to represent the mysterious reality are significant. His style is rich in powerful imagery, antitheses, paradoxes and oxymorons. For example, his Christmas hymn praises "eternity in the moment, summer in winter, day at night, heaven on earth, God in man", and he prays: "O thou great infant, whose all-embracing birth lifts earth to heaven and brings heaven down to earth!" He is also fond of hyperbole. In the *Hymn to the Name of Jesus* he declares: "Sweet name, in each of thy syllables dwell a thousand blissful Arabies, a thousand hills of incense and ten thousand Paradises." Strange as they may seem, these stylistic tricks are not unsuited to his subjects. Divine reality can only be alluded to in these terms, and even paradoxes and hyperboles lose their force in face of the divine wealth and grandeur. Human superlatives do not reach the divine positive, and human antitheses are dissolved in the divine unity.

In his poetry Crashaw reconciled this world and the next. He wrote poems about nature full of genuine feeling; a rare thing for this century. The verses in which he sketches an ideal picture of female beauty—a beauty that owes all its claims to nature, not to art—are quite delightful. The poem entitled *On Two Green Apricots which Mr Crashaw Sent to Cowley* is full of joy in earthly things. So the baroque joy in the world is not alien to Crashaw. But while other poets of this age saw such a contradiction between worldly pleasure and heavenly joy that they thought they had to choose between the two, and either as religious men despised the world or as worldly men despised heaven, Crashaw made a conscious attempt to embrace both. He could only conceive heavenly joy through and with earthly joy. He sees Mary ascend gloriously into heaven, which is "a piece of heavenly earth", and the Holy Ghost receives the beloved with whispered words of love: "Rise, my fair one, my spotless one! Winter is past, and the rain over. Spring has come, the flowers are budding. Only thou art missing here."

Milton (1608–74)

Milton learnt from Crashaw and far surpassed him; but the great Puritan was scarcely ever able to attain that harmony between the earthly and the heavenly which so delights us in the Catholic poet. On the one hand, with his strict morality and Old Testament piety, Milton is a true representative of English Puritanism in its noblest and purest form; on the other, his love for the sensuously beautiful and the purely human make him a legitimate heir to the Renaissance. He could not be both these things at the same time, and as a result there remained in his make-up "an unresolved tension between his humanism and his Puritanism, between the call of Greece and the influence of the Hebrew tradition" (Hutchinson). We can even feel in Milton a certain sense of cramp, which caused his pride and lack of humour. It has been said of him that he is one of those writers who inspire more respect than love.

His greatest work is *Paradise Lost*. In sonorous periods,

which extend through many lines of blank verse, this epic tells of the fall of man and his banishment from Eden. The main theme is the everlasting struggle between light and darkness. To portray it, the poet uses means which appeal more to the emotions and to the ear than to the eye. He also masters the artistic difficulty of representing in plastic form supernatural beings, whether angels or demons, and of portraying Adam and Eve before the fall and other realities outside human experience. Delightfully idyllic pictures alternate with grandiose scenes. The lofty figures of the spiritual world make a powerful appeal to the imagination. Satan's character is drawn best; here we have no laughable devil but a fearful giant.

In *Paradise Lost*, as in his work as a whole, Milton's purpose is not merely to entertain as a poet, but to teach as a prophet or, in his own words, "to justify God's ways to men". So he loads the epic with long theological digressions and discussions. Why did the fall of man take place? Because God created him free. How does God treat fallen man? He turns evil to good through the redemption. Behind the historical facts in which he believes Milton sees a deeper meaning. The fall and the redemption, which took place once in history, continue to take place in every age and in every individual. The struggle between Satan and Christ goes on still in every human soul. To fight bravely in this struggle is more heroic than to perform great deeds in war.

This heroic morality impels the poet to interpret traditional Christianity in an extremely personal way. Milton's belief that man can achieve salvation solely by subjecting his passions to the commands of reason is almost Pelagian. Not that he denies the necessity of divine grace, but it receives less emphasis than the need for self-control. The frequent allusions to pagan mythology in Milton are more than mere conventional ornaments; they indicate the underlying influence of non-Christian currents of thought. Neo-Platonic and rationalist elements are unmistakably present. Like the Arians, Milton seems to be denying Christ's divinity. God the Father, more given to uttering threats than to showing mercy, betrays more Old Testament than New Testament characteristics.

The defects of matter and form in *Paradise Lost* become still more prominent in the shorter epic, *Paradise Regained*. It portrays Christ's victory over Satan. It is characteristic of the Puritan poet that the subject he chose was the temptation of Jesus in the wilderness. "For Milton, the redemption was accomplished not on the cross but in the wilderness; it is not a mystery of love, but the triumph of reason over the passions, and Christ is not the son of God who sacrifices himself to divine justice, but the man who resists temptation" (Hutchinson). The paradise that was lost when Adam yielded to Satan's temptation was regained when Christ withstood the temptation of the same spirit.

Throughout his life Milton fought for political and religious freedom. His epic and lyric poetry served this aim just as much as his treatises and pamphlets. His object was preaching and propaganda. The real strength of his art lies not in objective creation but in subjective confession, not in the epic but in the lyric.

Even his drama *Samson Agonistes*, which borrows its subject from the Old Testament and its form from Greek tragedy, is really a lyric poem. In the blind prisoner Samson the poet portrays himself. He, too, wanted to free his people, and his struggle, too, was in vain. Disappointment at the defeat of the Puritan cause, anger at the Philistines of his own day, hope of final victory and triumph even in death: these are the dominant notes in this poem, whose power was enhanced still further by Handel's music.

Milton's lyrical gift was fully developed even in his youth. When he was only twenty-one he laid the Horatian ode *Hymn on the Morning of Christ's Nativity* as a gift from the heavenly Muse at the feet of the holy Infant. An ecstatic experience, hinted at in the introduction, inspires him to a hymn of joy. Enthusiastically he calls on the choirs of angels to join in with cymbals and trumpets. He casts a glance, not without regret, at the disappearing world of pagan beauty, but its seductive brilliance pales when suddenly a powerful light shines through the darkness. The expectant silence of the universe is shattered by heavenly music, whose harmony unites heaven and earth. But this is only the beginning of that glory which will not be perfected until the Last Day. The child now smiling in the manger must be crucified. The old dragon, although in fetters, still rages. But the old gods and demons are already in flight. The stanzas surge on with the full, deep sound of the organ, which the poet could play well. As always in Milton, the musical appeal of the poetry outweighs the visual. In the middle of the ode occurs the cosmic picture of the harmony of the spheres, which fills the universe with its loud notes and gripping rhythm.

Milton's sonnets differ substantially in form from the traditional models. Instead of weaving a musical pattern they build up powerfully to the climax of the last line. Their passionate rhythm corresponds to the baroque spirit. In the angry sonnet *On the Recent Slaughter in Piedmont,* which embraces the cause of the persecuted Waldensians, there are echoes of the psalms and prophets of the Old Testament. Other sonnets are addressed to persons; for example, the heartfelt one *To the Lady Margaret Ley,* the pious one on his deceased friend Mrs Thompson and the deeply moving one on his dead wife. The most beautiful and greatest of Milton's sonnets is the one *On His Blindness.* Seldom has Christian fortitude in the patient bearing of grievous suffering found such lofty expression as here:

> When I consider how my light is spent,
> E're half my days, in this dark world and wide,
> And that one Talent which is death to hide,
> Lodged with me useless, though my Soul more bent
> To serve therewith my Maker, and present
> My true account, least he returning chide,
> Doth God exact day-labour, light deny'd,

I fondly ask; But patience to prevent
That murmur, soon replies, God doth not need
Either man's work or his own gifts, who best
Bear his mild yoak, they serve him best, his State
Is Kingly. Thousands at his bidding speed
And post o're Land and Ocean without rest:
They also serve who only stand and waite.

The poet begins with a long dragging sentence whose main verb does not come until right at the end, in the eighth line. With hesitant steps the blind man gropes for the meaning of his enforced inactivity. His thoughts struggle forward with difficulty, and the broad stream of his words is given further weight by the way the sense overruns the lines. Patience personified answers comfortingly in short, pithy sentences which in content as well as form make an effective contrast to the plaintive yearning of the first part of the poem. This stylistic tension, an expression of pathos in thought and emotion, is characteristic of Milton and of baroque literature as a whole. The whole reaches a climax in the splendid majesty of the concluding line. The verse refers to the spiritual beings always in the presence of God, whose peace forms a contrast with the restlessness of the messengers hastening in all directions, and at the same time to the poet, condemned to inactivity. It is a moving testimony of surrender to God's will.

Bunyan (1628–88)

To the literary masterpieces written in captivity belong, by the side of Boethius' *Comfort of Philosophy*, More's *Dialogue of Comfort* and Cervantes' *Don Quixote*, the two main works of John Bunyan: his autobiography and the *Pilgrim's Progress*. This uneducated tinker is, after the erudite Milton, the most important literary representative of Puritanism.

It is surprising that the Puritans produced writers at all. They entertained a deep distrust of all products of the poetic imagination. Poetry was regarded as empty, deceitful and unhealthily exciting; the truth was only to be found in the

Bible. Poetry either had the same aims as the Bible, in which case it was superfluous, or different ones, in which case it was dangerous. So, in the preface to *Pilgrim's Progress*, Bunyan felt bound to make excuses for his book. He says that he is not trying to gain fame as a writer; what he has written, he has written "before the eyes of God". His only purpose is not entertainment but edification.

Bunyan's autobiography tells us about his spiritual development. The full title of the book is *Grace Abounding to the Chief of Sinners*. It has been said that in its heartfelt emotion, if not in rhetorical eloquence, Bunyan's autobiography is reminiscent of St Augustine's Confessions. We read in it of a struggle between heaven and hell whose violence corresponds to the worth of the human soul, which is more valuable than the whole world. Amid storms of depression, temptation and mortal terror a soul finds salvation. As Reinhold Schneider says, Bunyan found out by experience that "the road to heaven leads through the gate of hell". When he lay at the bottom of the abyss, light from above suddenly broke in upon him. "Thy justice is in heaven." He realized that his confidence should not be based on his inner conflicts or on his state of mind, but on an objective fact, the victory of Christ. "It is a good thing to kneel down and hold Christ in our arms before God." Bunyan became a Baptist preacher, fought with Cromwell's Ironsides, and after the political collapse of Puritanism spent twelve years in prison for preaching without a licence.

This period of imprisonment produced *The Pilgrim's Progress from this World to the Next*. Apart from the Bible, it has gone through more editions than any other book in English literature, and has been translated into 122 languages. The German translation reached over fifty editions in the last hundred years alone. The work delighted men like Melville and Macaulay. Abraham Lincoln knew whole passages of it by heart; Bernard Shaw thought highly of it because of its extremely unconventional tone.

Pilgrim's Progress is no dull work of edification, but a book full of religious dynamite. It gives a warning against any merely intellectual approach to Christianity. "The soul of religion is the practice of it." Christ "lays weight not on knowledge, but on accomplishment." There is such a thing as knowledge without action. A man may have the knowledge of an angel and yet not be a Christian. Christianity is not just a doctrine; it is a way of life. Nor is it to be confused with morality. Bunyan points out emphatically that Christianity and middle-class respectability are by no means the same thing. He represents a sternly ascetic, militant Christianity of uncompromising radicalism. He can tolerate no half-measures. As Andrew Lang says, "For him there is no other task but that of staying on the straight and narrow path and reaching the heavenly Jerusalem."

Pilgrim's Progress is not a dry allegory, but living symbolism. Bunyan tells his story in simple, unadorned English that makes no claim to brilliance of style and yet possesses a power that more carefully polished language often lacks. The tinker was not thinking of style when he wrote. All he wanted to do was to bring to life before his reader's eyes certain definite pictures which he himself saw as clearly as if he were Christian on the road instead of Bunyan in prison. He performed this task so skilfully that we too can sense the green grass of the Delectable Mountains beneath our feet, and feel the horror when the darkness of the Valley of the Shadow of Death envelops the pilgrim. Characters and scenes are portrayed with such vividness, humour, eloquence and, when the occasion demands it, tenderness, that we think of them as old acquaintances and events we have experienced ourselves. With its dramatic tension, experience of life and knowledge of human nature, *Pilgrim's Progress* became a real folk-story, which gives equal delight to children and grown-ups, the learned and the ignorant, Protestants and Catholics. It has been said that few nations possess a Christian folk-story so rich in poetic vision.

GERMANY

Bidermann (1578–1639)

In the Jesuit drama we meet what Günther Müller has called "a sphere of activity which in fertility as well as intellectual and poetic creativeness far outweighs anything the literary history of the period can point to in other departments of literature." The most gifted writer for the Jesuit stage was Father Jakob Bidermann, a versatile and fertile writer from Ehingen in Württemberg. Müller calls him "the first great baroque dramatist of Germany; the poet who boldly lifted the Jesuit drama from the relatively narrow confines of the school stage into the wider world of the public theatre." Another critic, W. Stammler, says "the enthusiastic, victoriously triumphant youth of the Jesuit order is personified in Bidermann's dramas."

What strikes us first about them is the many burlesque and comic scenes, their abundance of life, their realism and their humour. But these things are only superficial; the entertainment of the audience is not the ultimate purpose of Bidermann's plays. Fundamentally they have the same aim in view as the *Spiritual Exercises* of St Ignatius of Loyola; they are in fact, in Müller's words, "dramatic sermons on the basic themes of the *Exercitia Spiritualia*. It is primarily the meditations of the 'first week' that are portrayed with unparalleled vividness by this exceptional dramatist in the decisions and destinies of typical individuals. All worldly reality only has any value in so far as it can be made to contribute directly to the glorification of God; there is always the lurking danger that beauty, brilliance, power and wealth may come to be desired for their own sake." In face of the changeability of everything earthly, again and again the warning rings out to renounce ephemeral goods. The whole world seethes round man and with its forces will carry him off or drag him down. The only answer is an unconditional either/or, a decision between heaven and earth. This is the central fact which dictates the dramatic economy of

Bidermann's plays. Their purpose is to convert men, to prise
them loose from the world. And in fact, as many contemporary
witnesses testify, the comic scenes of these plays made audi-
ences laugh, and the serious scenes brought them first to tears
and finally to the decision to alter their lives.

Bidermann's first play is the Latin *Cenodoxus*. The chief
character, the world-famous scholar of Paris University, is
outwardly pious and humble, but inwardly ruled by vanity
and ambition. Again and again he has to choose between his
guardian angel and his self-love, which are at odds with each
other. But even on his death-bed he tries to win admiration as
an exemplary Christian. While disciples and friends are organ-
izing a solemn funeral for the dead man, Christ, the judge of
the world, condemns the hypocrite's soul to eternal damnation
and Cenodoxus plunges down to hell. A ghastly miracle causes
the corpse of the celebrated professor to sit up in its coffin on
the bier and announce its damnation to the terrified people.
The scholar's disciple, Bruno, is so horrified by the event that
he enters a monastery. The weighty conclusion makes it im-
pressively clear that hypocrisy is hateful to God and that his
judgement is infallible. Cenodoxus' sin did not lie in his
actions, but solely in his mental attitude. The play was performed in Augsburg, Paris and Ypres, and strongly influenced
contemporaries.

Like *Cenodoxus*, *Philemon Martyr*, too, borrows its theme
from an old legend about a saint. Philemon, an actor in the
Egyptian town of Antinoë, knows nothing but the pleasure of
dressing up and the "joys of the gullet and the belly", which
he describes as his gods. When the persecution under Diocletian breaks out, he sees among the Christians examples of
the martyr's courage but also of cowardice. The frightened
deacon Apollonius strikes upon the idea of hiring Philemon
to make the pagan sacrifice instead of himself. The actor
accepts the task with pleasure. This acting, however, becomes
unexpectedly earnest: through grace Philemon is so changed
inwardly that he becomes a Christian and refuses to make the

sacrifice. He is already being led to execution when the people recognize the popular actor and shout their applause. But Philemon persists in his profession of faith. The remorseful Apollonius makes himself known and the two of them are executed. A miracle at Philemon's grave converts the pagan governor, and he introduces Christianity in his province. In our day Bernt von Heiseler has given fresh life to this play of Bidermann's.

How firmly Bidermann believes in the ability of man to direct his life sensibly by the exertion of his will is shown by his play *Joseph*. The hero is torn this way and that by misfortune and good fortune, but keeps his mind firmly fixed on God, whose commands he tries to carry out in everything. *Joannes Calybita* expresses most strongly the disregard of the ascetic will for the self and all natural affections. On the other hand, *Jacobus Usurarius* shows the avaricious usurer being saved by the intercession of the Mother of God. The theme is always the choice between this world and the next, both in Bidermann's dramas and in his other work. The epic *Herodias* portrays the biblical story of the slaughter of the innocents as a fight to the death between heaven and hell. Bidermann's *Epigrams* and *Heroic Letters* express with polished lyrical art the same heaven-orientated spirituality.

Spee (1591–1635)

That pastoral aims need not be injurious to the artistic standard of a literary work is demonstrated not only by Bidermann's dramas but also by the books of a fellow-Jesuit, Friedrich von Spee. Admiration for the successes which St Francis Xavier had achieved as a missionary in India had drawn the young nobleman into the Society of Jesus. The poems in which Spee celebrated his hero Xavier reflect his own heroic zeal for souls: "Souls, souls must I have." Dangers and obstacles frighten him no more than they did the apostle of India and Japan. This attitude is the key to all his literary work.

Spee gained his greatest fame with his Latin book *Cautio criminalis*, which occupies an important place in the history of jurisprudence. It was directed against trials for witchcraft, a crying evil which, supported by ecclesiastical and secular authorities, had spread more and more since the end of the Middle Ages and in the seventeenth century had reached a dreadful climax. Almost everywhere Spee had been he had encountered the horrors of the persecution of witches. He himself had comforted many victims as their confessor; he knew the physical and mental torture they went through and that they were innocent. It was essential to show up these trials for the madness they were. In the *Cautio criminalis,* Spee addressed, as the title says, "the authorities of the German nation, councillors and confessors of princes, commissioners, inquisitors, judges, advocates, priests and preachers", in an effort to stir their consciences. "It is the duty of priests to bark not only at ordinary people, but also at nobles and princes, and to wake them from sleep, when a danger arises in the night." With unexampled courage Spee reminds princes sharply that they themselves will be called to account for the judicial murders which their judges and witchcraft commissioners carry out. Sometimes he writes factually, sometimes angrily and sometimes ironically, but always freshly, full-bloodedly, grippingly and with compelling logic. The book is a stylistic masterpiece, a thrilling defence of outraged human dignity.

The *Cautio criminalis* provoked at first only opposition and indignation. So old and firmly-rooted a superstition could not yield to reason overnight. Only towards the end of the seventeenth century did the *Cautio criminalis* find a hearing, especially in Protestant and rationalist circles. The Dutch pastor Balthasar Bekker praises the *Cautio* repeatedly in his famous book *The Enchanted World*, gives an excerpt from it and ends by saying that it "deserves to be printed in all the languages of Europe and to be read by persons of every rank". Spee's book was in fact translated into German, Flemish, Polish and French. The jurist Christian Thomasius, who at first declared that he would "stake his life" on the traditional doctrine about witches, was converted by reading the *Cautio*; "scales fell from his eyes", and he praised the book as "a completely destructive criticism of witchcraft trials". Leibniz testifies that the *Cautio* had done a great deal of good.

Spee's *Golden Book of Virtue* demonstrates how the religious life can be deepened by daily contemplation and the practice of the three divine virtues. It adheres to the tradition of Jesuit ascetic writing, but gives the old truth a new look. In form it is a dialogue between spiritual director and penitent, interspersed with poems and stories. The *Golden Book of Virtue* won great esteem among both Catholics and Protestants. Leibniz praised it as "one of the most solid and moving devotional books", wished to see it in the hands of every Christian and presented copies of it to various princes. It has often been reprinted right up to our own day.

In complete accordance with the spirit of the baroque age, Spee would like to see music and art employed in the praise of God and the care of souls:

> What a pleasure it will be to hear a splendid High Mass, in which all kinds of instruments are employed to make music— organ, drums, trombones, horns, strings and voices—and which is celebrated with stately ceremonies, vestments, incense, candles and servers! How fine it is to think that all this pomp and splendour impresses itself on our minds and thus remains within us for the eternal praise of God! Sometimes I feel as if all my blood is surging up in joy when I see a beautiful procession organized to honour God, or when I hear stately music in church, with the organ thundering and all the bells ringing together, or big guns being fired with frighteningly loud reports, or when High Mass is celebrated with great pomp and splendour.

The great use made by Spee of music and poetry in his pastoral work is brought vividly home to us by a pleasant anecdote which also provides a good example of improvisation. Spee once met on a journey a woman who was singing an unbecoming song. Without any embarrassment he went up to her, praised the tune and asked about the words. The woman blushed, but the Jesuit assured her charmingly that, he, too, was a music-lover and would write fresh words for her which would suit the tune better: and he really did write new verses for the old melody on the spot; they gave moving expression to remorse for sins. He sang them to the woman until she and all the bystanders knew them by heart. They were all so delighted with the song that it was often sung afterwards in the district.

The hymns which Spee wrote and himself set to music are not just everyday lyrics, but real poetry. In his collection *Better than the Nightingale,* the songs sound, as it says in the preface, "sweet and pleasant and genuinely poetic", and better than any nightingale. He praises the creator in lark and bee, wind and water, moon and stars. The German Romantic poet Eichendorff considered that no poet had listened to the hidden voices of nature with so much understanding as Spee. Joy, exultation and thanks are the keynotes of his devotion, and even when a note of unfathomable melancholy creeps in, it is one of incomparable sweetness. Some of the lyrics in this collection, it is true, are strongly influenced by the style of the period and the taste for pastoral poetry, but most of them have a lasting quality that has caused *Better than the Nightingale* to be reprinted again and again.

Spee is also the author of a third of the hymns printed anonymously in the hymn-book published by the Jesuits of Cologne in 1625. There are more than a hundred of these anonymous hymns, and many of them are still sung today; for example, the Advent hymn *O Heiland reiss die Himmel auf* ("O Saviour, open up the heavens") and the carols *Als ich bei meinen Schafen wacht* ("As I kept watch beside my sheep") and *Von Himmel hoch, o Engel, kommt* ("Come, ye Angels, from heaven on high").

Friedrich von Spee is unquestionably the greatest religious lyric poet of seventeenth-century Germany. Only Paul Gerhardt and Angelus Silesius can be compared to him, and they both owe a great deal to him. As Zoepfl says, "In Spee are exemplified the best qualities of the early baroque age: intensified feeling, tautened will-power and courageous action." From the formal point of view his poems show a tremendous advance; they anticipate in practice what Opitz[1] achieved in theory.

Angelus Silesius (1624–77)

Angelus Silesius was able to build on Spee's achievement in the field of the hymn. He came from Breslau and his real name was Johannes Scheffler. He was personal physician to the emperor Ferdinand III, was converted from Protestantism to Catholicism, and became a priest. His collection of poems entitled *Heilige Seelenlust oder Geistliche Hirten-Lieder der in ihren Jesum verliebten Psyche* ("The Soul's Delight, or Pastoral Songs of the Spirit in Love with Jesus") is centred round the love song to Jesus. The Song of Songs provided the content, pastoral poetry the form. But Scheffler was also influenced by the Protestant and Catholic hymn, the Latin hymn and, above all, by Spee's *Better than the Nightingale.* His poems are so heartfelt and tender that the soul's rapture could hardly find stronger expression. They often become sensuously sweet, but Silesius is also capable of a lofty heroic tone; for example, in the triumphant *Dich, König, loben wir* ("Thee, O King, we praise"). One of his best hymns is *Ich will Dich lieben, meine Stärke* ("I will love thee, thou my strength"). Angelus Silesius influenced not only the Catholic baroque lyric, but also the Pietist hymn. Tersteegen incorporated fifteen of Scheffler's hymns in his collection, and two of them are still found in evangelical hymn-books today.

More important than *The Soul's Delight* are the polished aphorisms of the *Cherubinische Wandersmann* ("The Cherubic

---

[1] Martin Opitz (1597–1639) was the Ronsard of German poetry. His *Buch von der deutschen Poeterey* (1624) laid the foundations of modern German prosody. (*Trans.*)

Pilgrim"). The author prefaces the work with a short sketch of the Church's mystical theology, in which he explains particularly that in the union of the soul with God the soul becomes through grace what God is by nature. Daring and unchristian as these bold epigrams sometimes sound, they all admit a Christian interpretation. Sometimes their concise formulation certainly does blur the distinction between creature and creator. Silesius' speculative mysticism draws on troubled springs such as Böhme, the Pseudo-Dionysius, Plotinus and Proklus, but it also takes over numerous expressions from mystics like Bernard of Clairvaux, Tauler, Ruysbroeck, Dionysius van Ryckel and John of the Cross.

The main theme of the *Cherubic Pilgrim* is the stripping of the ego of all dependence on earthly things as the way to the mystical union, the apotheosis of man. Man must first become conscious that he is called to a higher destiny:

A heart that is satisfied with time and place does not know its own infinity.

Man, be essential; for when the world passes away, the transitory disappears and the essence remains.

The man who does not lift his mind above himself does not deserve to be a man.

Man's self-knowledge only becomes complete through his knowledge of God. There are two ways of knowing God: analogy and negation:

God is a spirit, a fire, an essence and a light; and yet again he is none of these things.

Angelus Silesius also often uses paradox as a means of grasping the complex reality of God:

Note that God has never exerted himself, nor rested; his work is rest, his rest is work.

The important thing is that man should attain to God after God has come down to man:

Heaven sinks down, and comes to join Earth; when will Earth ascend, and rise to join Heaven?

The presupposition of any union of man with God is love:

Man, what thou lovest, that wilt thou become; God wilt thou be, if thou lovest God, Earth, if thou lovest Earth.

Many of the epigrams are concerned with the immanence of God in the soul and the resting of the natural being in the divine being:

I do not wish for power or art, wisdom, wealth or glory, but only to rest in my father's bosom.

Angelus Silesius calls man to cooperate with God's grace and to the imitation of Christ:

If Christ is born a thousand times in Bethlehem and not in thee, then art thou lost for ever.

The Cross on Golgotha cannot release thee from sin if it is not set up in thy heart, too.

The ripeness of these epigrams produces the impression of soaring. As Günther Müller has said, "Scheffler possesses a plastic power hardly ever displayed before. In his verses, his vision attains a physical outline and movement which make the content of the lines more than mere abstract statements. . . . Scheffler's unique art does not expound a system of mystical theology; it makes points of light glow in the darkness, so that his work has the effect of a string of stars in a dark sky. . . . In the most perfect of these epigrams there are hints of much more, and of far profounder things, than what is actually said."

The *Cherubinische Wandersmann* influenced not only Catholic writers, but also Protestants such as Gottfried Arnold, Gerhard Tersteegen and Friedrich Rückert.

Gerhardt (1607–76)

The third great hymn-writer of seventeenth-century Germany is Paul Gerhardt, the greatest lyric poet produced by the German Protestant Church. His lyrics are distinguished by their purity of form. They are smooth and melodiously balanced. Gerhardt has a happy sense of rhythm and sound, and at the same time a spring of warm and pure emotion and a heart-warming imagination. His is a profoundly peace-loving nature, and images of peace and happiness dominate his work. The difference between Gerhardt and Luther has been rightly emphasized; for Luther, the world is full of storms and tempests; in Gerhardt, the world lies in continual sunshine. Luther struggles against the devil; for Gerhardt, death and hell have long lost their power. In Luther, the community cries out to God; in Gerhardt, the individual speaks. But this picture of Gerhardt needs some modification.

Although most of Gerhardt's hymns are written in the first person, they are not subjective but universally valid. A good example is *O Haupt voll Blut und Wunden* ("O bloodstained, wounded head"). This contemplative lyric addressed to Christ crucified is not an entirely original creation, but an adaptation of a thirteenth-century poem by Arnulf von Löwen. Here is a prose translation of it: "When I must depart, do not depart from me; when I must suffer death, suffer it in my stead; when fear clutches at my heart, snatch me from its grasp by virtue of your fear and pain."

That is the personal utterance of an individual heart, but it is also so universal in its appeal that the poem still can and does serve to express the emotions of us all. Gerhardt's hymns are real community hymns; they are so devoid of any purely private note that they make no contribution to the poet's biography.

We know little about Gerhardt's life from other sources either. Legend fills the gaps left by the documents. But the little we know for certain is enough to make it clear that, rather surprisingly, Gerhardt's life was by no means so idyllic as his hymns. The godliness expressed by his verses was not easily attained, and Christian joy did not fall into his lap. Anyone who thought of this Lutheran pastor as a harmless and naïve person will have been undeceived by the words under his portrait in the church at Lübben: *Theologus in cribro Satanae versatus*; "a theologian shaken about in Satan's sieve". Gerhardt lived through the upheaval and devastation of the Thirty Years' War. His children died and he lost his wife, too. In Berlin he was deprived of his ministry by the Great Elector and banished from the country because he was unwilling to bow to the new religious decree on conscientious grounds. He certainly had his share of suffering.

But in all his sufferings he never doubted God's justice and goodness; on the contrary, he overcame the suffering of this world with a firm and unshakable faith. He possessed the same sort of confidence that inspired Thomas More in his dungeon, and it is expressed in the same sort of imagery. His triumphant, heartfelt cheerfulness finds its best expression in the *Sommer-Lied* ("Summer Song"):

> Geh aus mein Herz und suche Freud
> In dieser lieben Sommerzeit
>   An deines Gottes Gaben:
> Schau an der schönen Garten Zier
> Und siehe, wie sie mir und dir
>   Sich ausgeschmücket haben.[2]

The next six stanzas describe vividly the beauties of summer; then the poet turns to praise of the creator and to contemplation of the heavenly paradise. Many of Gerhardt's hymns take the form of songs of praise, and today Catholic as well as Protestant congregations still praise the Lord in Gerhardt's words. His carol *Ich steh an deiner Krippe hier* ("I stand here at your crib") and the hymn to the heart of Jesus, *O Herz des Königs aller Welt* ("O heart of the King of all the World"), are also sung in both Catholic and Protestant churches.

Gryphius (1616–64)

Andreas Gryphius is a Lutheran like Paul Gerhardt, but the whole tone of his poetry is quite different. He, too, went through the sufferings of the age and shook under the blows

---

[2] Go out, my heart and find your joy, now that summer is here, in the gifts of God: look at the flowers in the gardens, and see how they have decked themselves out for you and me.

of fate, but while, in spite of life's miseries, Gerhardt continued to love the world, Gryphius felt compelled to reject earthly things and to make a stern decision in favour of the eternal as opposed to the ephemeral.

In the *Kirchhofsgedanken* ("Churchyard Thoughts"), he sees in imagination the skeletons, the rotting corpses and the worms devouring them. The *Sonn-und Feiertagssonette* ("Sonnets for Sundays and Holidays") are grim meditations on the total collapse of human existence, which is described with brutal frankness and whose pains are piled on top of each other into a sum total of human fears. This view of life excites the cry of fear: "Let me not perish like a burnt-out candle!" This Silesian measured the whole of life by the standard of the absolute. His poetry knows only two realms: this world which is lost forever and the salvation of the next:

> Ade, verfluchte Welt! Du See voll rauher Stürme!
> Glück zu, mein Vaterland! Das stete Ruh im Schirme
> Und Schutz und Friede hält, du ewig lichter Schloss.[3]

Again and again the preacher's theme recurs: "All is vanity!" The ode *Vanitas! Vanitatum Vanitas!* begins with the words:

> The splendour of the earth must turn into smoke and ashes.
> No rock, no brass can last.

This central thought is illustrated in a series of examples and images. The Renaissance desire for fame is marked out particularly for a thrust:

> The fame for which we strive, and which we think immortal,
> is only a delusion.

Gryphius is dominated by the conviction that "no power or crown can last for ever". The conclusion of the *Vanitas* ode demands that man should turn away from transitory appearances and devote himself to the eternal reality.

The tension between the reality of earthly life and the

[3] Farewell, accursed world! Thou sea of savage storms! Hail, my Fatherland! Thou that dost possess eternal rest and safety and peace, like an ever-lit castle!

reality of eternal life is felt as something sad. Gryphius does not see the one reality as a symbol of the other. For him the horrors of earth obscure the bliss of heaven; the pressure of the world's reality even tries to push aside the reality of faith and to make it invisible: "In our misery, it seems as if faith were extinct and dead in us." In spite of this, the poet remains firmly convinced that the two realities are not of equal importance. Thus amid threats of war he can celebrate Christmas night, when "peace on earth" is proclaimed. It is a paradoxical situation:

> But if through thee, O God, I am at peace with God,
> I can be happy, even if the world passes away.

A new note enters his work here, and we realize that Gryphius also knows the joy of the redeemed. The night of Christ's birth brings a light that defies all earthly darkness:

> Night, that is more than light! Night lighter than the day! Night brighter than the sun, in which the light was born, the light that God, who is light himself and dwells in light, chose for himself!

So, in Gryphius, too, the sorrow of the world is finally overcome by faith.

It is extraordinary that the same Gryphius who uttered such grim words in his lyric poetry about the deceit of this ephemeral world can, in other works, celebrate earthly pleasures with great enjoyment. The author of the tragedy *Leo Armenius*, which seeks to demonstrate in the fall of the Byzantine emperor the fragility of earthly greatness, also wrote a number of juicy and humorous comedies which testify to his love of life.

The spiritual extremes embraced by Gryphius' work are paralleled by its outward variety. In creative power and versatility Gryphius is the greatest writer of the German baroque period. Everything he wrote—his Latin epic, *The Mount of Olives*, on the passion of Christ, his lyric poetry, his epigrams and satires, his tragedies, comedies and festival plays, his translations from Dutch, Italian and French—reflects an exceptional literary talent. There are many dusty echoes of humanistic academicism, with its insistence on established patterns and set rules, but through the baroque rhetoric with its conventional similes and mythological ornaments the true voice of the spirit can be heard. The language heaves under the poet's heart throbs, and the hindrances of the form only serve to make the dammed-up flood of feeling rush on with greater force. This is particularly true of Gryphius' lyric poetry, of his Pindaric odes and his sonnets. Passion often threatens to split the strict form; indeed, in the Hell-sonnet it does split it, and this poem can scarcely be called a sonnet. But this quite exceptional intensity of feeling is accompanied by a strong and disciplined intellect whose favourite form of expression is the dialectic of pointed antitheses.

Gryphius' best work is to be found in his dramas. We are only interested here in the religious pieces, that is, the tragedies. They show the influence of the Jesuit drama. As in Bidermann's plays, the action centres round the decision which man must take in the conflicts of life, and whose results are inescapable. Gryphius translated *Felicitas*, the Latin drama of martyrdom by the French Jesuit Causinus. Its heroine is the Christian mother who saw her seven sons put to death one after the other and encouraged each of them to be true to his faith, until finally she herself was killed.

Such stories, which show man in extreme situations, fascinated Gryphius. He himself wrote three martyr-plays full of dramatic tension and gripping speeches: *Katharina von Georgien oder Bewährete Beständigkeit* ("Catherine of Georgia or Fortitude Maintained"), *Grossmütiger Rechtsgelehrter oder sterbender Ämilius Paulus Papinianus* ("The Brave Jurist or the Death of Aemilius Paulus Papinianus") and the drama on a contemporary subject, *Die ermordete Majestät oder Carolus Stuardus* ("Murdered Majesty or Charles Stuart"), which deals with Charles I, who had just died on the scaffold. The action of these plays is inserted emphatically in the context of eternity, and this gives meaning to the element of sheer horror in them.

More touching than the heroic persistence in virtue depicted in these plays is the psychological progress through a series of temptations, struggles and defeats to final victory, as portrayed in the tragedy *Cardenio und Celinde oder unglücklich Verliebte* ("Cardenio and Celinde or the Unlucky Lovers").

Vondel (1587–1679)

Gryphius learnt much about the drama from the Dutch writer Joost van den Vondel, whose *Netherlandish Art of Poetry* was an epoch-making book. Gryphius translated into German Vondel's play *The Gibeonites*, which deals with the destruction of the house of Saul by David; and Vondel's tragedy *Maria Stuart*, which put on the stage an event from very recent history, was the model for Gryphius' *Carolus Stuardus*. Joost van den Vondel, who died in Amsterdam at the age of ninety-two, was born in Cologne. He did not break all links with his native city when he settled in Holland. He dedicated to the City of Cologne his religious play about St Ursula and the eleven thousand maidens.

The son of Anabaptist parents, in 1641 he became a Catholic, and his work is entirely Catholic in spirit. Vondel is Holland's greatest dramatist; his plays represent the high water mark of Dutch baroque and are still performed today in Dutch theatres. The ripeness of the thought and the force of the language make them extremely effective. In form they are reminiscent, like the plays of Vondel's greater contemporary Calderon, of the medieval mystery play. In spite of Vondel's delight in inspiring horror and fear, Christian optimism is always the dominant note.

The best of his 32 tragedies are *Luzifer,* a play about the creation of the world which has been described as "the masterpiece of European baroque literature" and influenced Milton's *Paradise Lost*; *Jephta,* a biblical tragedy; *Samson Agonistes,* which influenced Milton's poem of the same name and the whole German drama of the seventeenth and eighteenth centuries; and a play about the apostles called *Peter and Paul*.

Vondel also wrote some didactic poems about the truths of religion, a miniature epic, *John the Baptist*, and a translation of the psalms. His most famous spiritual poem, *Der Kreuzberg* ("Calvary"), has been described as offering "with the heavy, trailing brocade of its imagery and rhymes a perfect example of the baroque style."

Abraham a Sancta Clara (1644–1709)

The blunt Swabian Ulrich Megerle, an Augustinian friar and provincial of his order, won a great reputation in Vienna as a preacher. Aristocrats and craftsmen, Catholics and Protestants alike were swept away by his words. Although he spoke the unvarnished truth to all classes of people, especially the upper classes, the emperor Leopold made him court preacher. Circumstances made Abraham a Sancta Clara—that was Megerle's name in religion—into a writer. He published his first work, *Merks Wien* ("Take Note, Vienna"), when the plague broke out in Vienna in 1679. His powerful summons, *Auf, auf, ihr Christen* ("Christians, Awake"), was occasioned by the danger that threatened from the Turks. These publications were followed by *Judas der Erzschelm* ("Judas the Arch-knave"), Abraham's main work. It fills four quarto volumes, and is a kind of encyclopaedia of vice illustrated by references to the life of Judas. Altogether Abraham's collected works fill twenty-one volumes. He exerted considerable influence on both Catholic and Protestant preachers and writers. Goethe praised him; Schiller saw in him "a splendid original genius who inspires respect" and imitates his style in the Capuchin's sermon in *Wallensteins Lager*; and Jean Paul called him "the father of all modern humorists".

CHAPTER III

THE NINETEENTH CENTURY

ROMANTICISM

De Maistre (1754–1821)

Joseph Marie, Count de Maistre, chancellor of Sardinia, ambassador in St Petersburg and Minister of State in Turin, achieved eminence not only as a diplomat and statesman, but also as a publicist and writer of wide-ranging interests. He championed the political ideals of early French Romanticism, and struggled against the Revolution and against Napoleon for a legitimate monarchy that was to be allied with the Papacy, still a temporal power. He praised earlier ages, in which society and Church had formed a unity; the goal of his endeavours was a theocratic and absolutist restoration.

De Maistre was one of those who, after the Enlightenment and the French Revolution, pointed out that the despised and persecuted Church is indispensable to the State and society. He wanted freedom for the Church *vis-à-vis* the State, but an increase of authority in the Church itself. Although he believed in the special mission of France, he rejected Gallicanism and was in favour of a close tie between France and the Papacy.

In his most important book, *Du Pape* ("Concerning the Pope"), he developed the idea of the infallibility of the pope in all its breadth and beauty, and praised the services rendered by Peter's chair to civilization and society. The book sees the cause of the break-up of all traditional relationships in the anti-clerical ideas of the age. "In spite of the weakness of its historical, philosophical and theological foundations, it became one of the most important pioneers of that unity of the Church which is fulfilled in the Vatican" (Lortz).

As a philosopher of history, De Maistre is full of prophetic vision, and has been described (by Paulhan) as "a real metaphysical and mystical genius." The long-lasting nature of his influence is attested by the fact that Leo XIII applied many of his ideas in his encyclicals. De Maistre is completely permeated by the Christian belief in providence. He is confident that everything that happens, however terrible it may be, contributes to the advancement of the world in accordance with God's will. This conception of the divine meaning of history is developed in a somewhat exaggerated way.

In the *St Petersburg Nights* De Maistre collected his leading ideas in the form of conversations. At times he writes earnestly, at others wittily, but always from the conservative point of view which knows the value of the Christian tradition.

Chateaubriand (1768–1849)

It was above all François René Vicomte de Chateaubriand who, together with De Maistre, Lamennais, Lacordaire and Montalembert, created by his writing a Catholic atmosphere in France after the destructive influence of the Enlightenment and the Revolution. He is the real founder of French Romanticism. This emotional and unstable Breton, who was endowed by nature with an overflowing imagination, began as a disciple of Rousseau and Voltaire. He witnessed the Revolution in Paris, explored the primitive forests and prairies of America, lived among the Indians, fought in the French émigré army, was wounded and fled to England. Illness and poverty, the death of his brother and sister on the guillotine, and that of his tenderly-loved mother and sister as a result of imprisonment and ill-treatment, all tore his heart. He turned to Christianity: one of the many emotional conversions which mark the Romantic age. His own words were, "I wept and believed."

Characteristic of this subjective, aesthetic approach to religion is Chateaubriand's book *Le Génie du Christianisme* ("The Genius of Christianity"), which appeared in 1802. Originally it was to be called "Concerning the Poetic and Moral Beauty of the Christian Religion" and was to be a poetic theology, an aesthetic of Catholicism. Chateaubriand's aim is to defend Christianity against its rationalist opponents. But he does not argue with the free-thinkers. He has no intention of trying to prove the truth of Christianity by rational means. He wants to move his readers, to employ "all the magic of the imagination and every kind of appeal to the heart" in order to show that of all religions Christianity is the most poetic, the most human and the most amiable. It furthered freedom, art and knowledge, to which the modern world is indebted for everything.

Although this approach misses the essential nature and real task of Christianity, it was important at that time to stress these aspects of it. The eighteenth century had cried down Christianity as tasteless and barbaric, despised it as hostile to beauty, and heaped mockery on its ritual, its ceremonies and its scriptures. By rehabilitating Christianity on these points the artist Chateaubriand became its most successful apologist. The *Genius of Christianity* admires the beauty of Gothic churches, organ music, and Gregorian chant, processions, the Bible and Christian literature. The Enlightenment had ridiculed everything that seemed to be opposed to reason as superstitious and absurd. Chateaubriand maintained on the contrary that the only things in life that are "beautiful, gentle and great" are the mysterious things. The irrational and the mysterious had re-asserted their rights.

That the *Genius of Christianity* should portray Christianity as the repository of beauty and defender of humanity and freedom was typically romantic. But it was precisely this which affected people at the time and won their hearts for the Catholic Church. In his memoirs Chateaubriand was able to boast without much exaggeration that with his book he had rebuilt Christianity on the ruins of the Enlightenment and the

Revolution, and jerked people out of the habits of thought of the eighteenth century. "He succeeded in striking just the right note, and in saying in an irresistible way the things most likely to win converts for Christianity in the widest circles of society" (Heiss).

Chateaubriand also published political and ecclesiastical works. "I am a supporter of the Bourbons from loyalty," he confessed, "a royalist by intellectual conviction, and a republican by taste and character." Other books of Chateaubriand's which deserve to be mentioned by name are *Les Martyrs ou le triomphe de la religion Chrétienne* ("The Martyrs, or the Triumph of Christianity"), a novel set in the time of Diocletian and showing the spiritual strength of Christianity, which triumphs over paganism, and *La Vie de Rancé*, a biography of the founder of the Trappists written at the suggestion of his confessor. With his thrilling rhetoric, brilliant style and magical skill with words, Chateaubriand was a stimulating influence in almost every field.

Manzoni (1785–1873)

What De Maistre and Chateaubriand were to France, the Milanese Count Alessandro Manzoni was to Italy: the leader of the Romantic movement, the opponent of the Enlightenment, and the herald of the awakening national consciousness and the Catholic revival. He, too, cherished rationalistic and revolutionary views in his youth. What he wrote in those days is of no significance. Only after his re-conversion to Catholicism did he gain the impetus which made him the greatest and most influential Italian writer of the nineteenth century.

The positive side of his earlier views—sympathy for the weak and oppressed, a democratic attitude and the eighteenth century's belief in humanity—he retained. The faith which he adopted was a liberal Catholicism. This spirit informs Manzoni's patriotic poems as well as his religious ones. Manzoni's Catholicism was by no means superficial.

In a letter to Fauriel in 1812 Manzoni said that he was at

that moment engaged on the first of the *Holy Hymns*, the *Resurrection*. The poem's name symbolizes the resurrection of the writer's faith. Yet this hymn is not an outpouring of personal feeling, but a picture of the faith which the poet now shares with all the faithful. The later *Holy Hymns* on feasts of the Church are just as objective: *The Name of Mary*, *Christmas*, *The Passion* and *Whitsun*. Biblical events are linked with the symbolism of the liturgy and religious usages. The poet addresses the community of the faithful, in order to remind them of the mystery of each feast. The dominant mood is the triumph of faith, the basic theme the transfiguration of the idea of the Church and religion through the influence of the Holy Ghost.

Manzoni was a man of strong emotions and religious temperament. He held the view that poetry must come from the heart, but he refrained from the direct expression of his feelings. For him, poetry was not, as it was for Wordsworth, "a spontaneous outpouring of powerful emotions", but the moulding of an objective form. It is characteristic of Manzoni that he wrote no personal lyrics. What distinguishes his verse is the carefully controlled emotion which gives the fiery rhythms of his poems their warmth. Thus, in his disciplined manliness, Manzoni is as far removed from stiff coldness as from sentimental exaggeration. This is particularly true of the *Holy Hymns*, whose solemn language is reminiscent of the prophets, the gospels and the psalms, and bears the stamp of universality. They are a landmark in the history of Italian literature.

One of Manzoni's most famous poems is the *Ode on the Fifth of May*. It is a meditation on the death of Napoleon, and poses the question whether his fame was genuine. Manzoni rejects force and oppression and repudiates fame won in war, but sees in Napoleon a tool of providence. Thus the patriotic ode, too, ends with the triumph of faith.

Manzoni's *Observations on Catholic Morality*, written in defence of Catholicism, provide evidence of his dialectical mentality. Like the *Holy Hymns*, they show that the roots of his faith were a profoundly ethical temperament, innate love of his fellow men and Christian charity. At the same time they provide the theoretical basis of his novel, *The Betrothed*. This great book delighted Goethe. It was, and still is, read avidly throughout Europe. Renzo, an honourable and good-natured silk-spinner of Lake Como, wants to marry the good Lucia, but is prevented from doing so by the intrigues of a violent feudal lord and the fear of the old priest Don Abbondio. The two lovers are torn apart, and their attempts to be re-united involve them both in innumerable exciting adventures. The base tricks of knaves alternate with deeds of heroic virtue. The story broadens out into a grand historical panorama when Manzoni tells of famine, war and pestilence, and brings on historical characters like the Cardinal-Archbishop of Milan, Federigo Borromeo. There is a happy ending, and the betrothed couple are finally married. They live happily in the midst of their children, to whom they impart the knowledge won from their own experience that "misfortune frequently comes because it has been deserved, but the most prudent and innocent behaviour is not enough to ward it off, and when it does come, deservedly or undeservedly, it can be softened by trust in God and made to yield a valuable lesson".

Novalis (1772–1801)

Although Friedrich von Hardenberg, who is known as Novalis, lived most of his life in the eighteenth century, he belongs to the nineteenth in spirit and in the influence exerted by his writing. His *Hymns to the Night* were written in 1800, and his *Christendom or Europe* was not published until 1826. As a Romantic, he was opposed to the Enlightenment, which buried essential religious impulses under a layer of rationalism; he lived in the mysterious twilight of fairy tales and myths, of dreams and night. His was a subjective and personal kind of religion; what he wanted above all was an emotional thrill. Brought up in the atmosphere of the Herrnhuter communities and influenced by Hemsterhuis, Böhme, Spinoza, Baader and

Zinzendorf, Novalis came to adopt a religion based on emotion rather than dogma, which yet draws sustenance from the Christian tradition.

Today Romantic piety is reproached "with blurring in an inadmissible way the boundary between God and the world. There is too much aesthetic sensibility and too little moral earnestness. The necessary distinction between state of mind and firm belief, eros and agape, vague nostalgia and genuine hope of immortality is completely absent" (Köberle). But behind the flood of fierce emotion there is an undeniable longing for the restoration of the original unity in God, for the reunion of things that have been separated: nature and mind, man and woman, man and animal, soul and world, dream and reality, Hellenism and Christianity, man and God. Novalis' *Fragments* were the fruit of this gnostic striving to see the unity which underlies everything. They express wonder at all the phenomena of life, nature, knowledge, art and religion. Novalis sees a divine secret concealed behind everything. But it also becomes clear that his faith was by no means of the child-like variety. He was a man of religious temperament, a seeker after God who considered that there were many possible ways to him and tied himself to none of them. He believed in a "religion of beauty", "an artists' religion", and said: "Religious doctrine is scientific poetry". Novalis' Catholic tendencies must be seen in the light of this attitude; they sprang from his aesthetic and philosophical striving for unity. "His inclination towards Catholicism was very marked; in fact probably no one did more than he to attract the young to the Catholic religion. Later on a defence of the Jesuits appeared in his collected works" (Steffens).

The best expression of his striving for unity is the essay *Christendom or Europe*. The French Revolution and the wars that followed it awoke in Novalis the consciousness of profound changes which permeates the whole essay. After a somewhat uncritical backward glance at the unified world of the Middle Ages, at "those dazzling times when Europe was one Christian land", and a survey of the age of cleavage and destruction, Novalis says: "Now the age of resurrection has come!" He sees "A new humanity", can feel already "the heart-beat of the new age" and "the first labour pains"; "let everyone prepare for the birth." What follows is really not a prognosis. It is a series of demands for a broader intellectual view, demands that have been repeated a century and a half later by writers like Ortega, Dawson, T. S. Eliot, Haecker, Jaspers and Ernst Jünger. The mark of the new age is a new unity which, as in the Middle Ages, unites harmoniously all human powers: unity of knowledge, unity of Europe, unity of religion.

Novalis regrets most of all the religious cleavage of the West. He says that Protestantism led to rationalism, enlightenment and deism. "The history of contemporary unbelief is worthy of note: it is the key to all the remarkable happenings of modern times." Novalis longs for the reunion of the separated Churches: "Christendom must regain its life and vigour, and form itself once again into *one* visible Church without regard for national frontiers. It must pour out the old cornucopia of blessings on the peoples once again."

Novalis' *Hymns to the Night* owe their origin to a personal experience: the death of his fiancée Sophie. To the poet it was the shattering experience considered necessary by the Pietists to enable man to win salvation. The longing to follow Sophie is expressed in images provided by Christian mysticism. The night of death opens on to a brighter light than the light of earth. In the centre of the starlight of the *Hymns* stands the image of Christ crucified, and from the heart of the Redeemer light streams, as from a sun, over the suffering world. Thus the *Hymns* proclaim the defeat of death by Christ and the fulfilment of all longing in the world to come. "Indestructible stands the cross—the triumphal standard of our race." But so many mythical and magical elements are mixed with these Christian elements that only in a limited sense can the *Hymns* be described as Christian literature. It is different with the

Spiritual Songs. They continue to hand on the tradition of Pietistic community singing. Some of them have won a place in Protestant hymn-books and are still sung in church today. However, they do not express the faith of the community, but simply what goes on in the soul of one individual devoted to Christ. Yet Novalis is no individualist, but a singer of brotherly fellowship, who rejoices that the union with Christ has brought him, too, back into the community of the disciples of Jesus. Nor are his eyes fixed only on the next world; he is a poet whose vision includes this earth in the redemption:

> Heaven is here with us on earth,
> We see it with the eye of faith;
> And it is also opened to those
> Who share our faith.

And again:

> From plant and stone and sea and light
> Shimmers his child-like countenance.

Here is a translation of the last stanza of the loveliest of the *Spiritual Songs*:

> Wherever I have him, is my fatherland; and every gift falls into my hand like an inheritance; long-missed brothers I find again in his disciples.

When Novalis died at the age of twenty-eight, his death seemed to his contemporaries, for all their grief, like a transfiguration. People saw something unearthly in him. Some called him a cherub; Tieck compared him with the apostle John, Friedrich Schlegel referred to him as a second Christ; Schleiermacher called him simply the "noble youth". Görres pronounced a more sober and accurate verdict on Novalis and his writing: "Even if his achievements did not attain the very highest rank, they were substantial."

Görres (1776–1848)

As a university teacher in Heidelberg, Görres praised the German Middle Ages; in Koblenz, as editor of the *Rheinische*

Merkur, he supported the struggle against Napoleon. After returning, in Strasbourg, to the faith of his childhood, he became professor of history in Munich and the spiritual leader of the German Catholic revival.

The goal of all his public activities was the renewal of Germany and Europe through Christianity. He was a man of uncompromising character, and in the *Rheinische Merkur* laid down the principle that the Church must either receive complete recognition or else be completely eradicated; there could be no half-measures. Görres defended the Church as a bulwark against the destructive contradictions of modern times, and the most reliable guardian of the most important traditions. This conviction forms the foundation of all his later works, whether they portray a medieval saint (*St Francis, a Troubadour*), glorify medieval architecture (*Cologne Cathedral and Strasbourg Minster*) or examine a medieval legend (*The Pilgrimage to Trier*). His innumerable articles for two Catholic periodicals, *Der Katholik* and *Historisch-Politische Blätter,* had a tremendous effect, thanks to the gripping quality of his prose. Görres' friend Clemens Brentano gave this verdict on them: "Not for centuries have Catholic matters been discussed so acutely, so boldly and with such imaginative fire."

Görres saw everything in a religious light, as is shown by the following excerpt from his *Political Writings,* in which he demands that God should stand at the centre of all our activity: "Man should do nothing without God; love for God should fill him, and enthusiasm for God should spur him on to all good works. God must be his very heart-beat, his deepest nerve, the source of all his joy in life."

Görres' most important work is to be found in the four volumes of his *Christian Mysticism.* The book was written in deliberate opposition to rationalism. Görres built on a historical foundation, but also wished to give a philosophical exposition of the material, and so produced "an attempt to describe systematically and logically all the phenomena of the inner life of the personality" (Dempf). His aim was to awaken understanding for the deeper experiences of the Christian spirit.

Görres handles an enormous mass of material, and displays an exceptional knowledge of history and amazing erudition in the field of hagiography. Montalembert, who heard Görres' lectures on Christian mysticism, confessed that they had provided him with the key to an unsuspected source of insight and enjoyable instruction.

In the lectures he gave at Munich on world history, Görres wished, as he himself explained, "to bring out the growth through struggle and strife of the Kingdom of God throughout history. The laws of this gradual development should stand out clearly, and since in these laws history has found its vivifying, inspiring and, above all, sanctifying principle, it will appear in its whole course as a widespread, thoroughly articulated and universally organized growth." These lectures had an immeasurable effect.

When the Prussian government, in the dispute over mixed marriages, incarcerated the Archbishop of Cologne, von Droste-Vischering, in the fortress of Minden, Görres took a hand in the violent struggle that followed with his *Athanasius*. This polemical work first reports the facts and establishes that the archbishop had acted with complete correctness. The book ends with a call to Catholics: "Band yourselves together firmly, for you all have the same goal: the complete and entire attainment of the solemnly promised religious freedom and of political and civil equality for Catholicism in all its aspects without risk or reservation." This inflammatory piece of writing awoke the community feeling and political consciousness of German Catholics. Here as always Görres wanted to be "a witness and fighter for eternal truth before a corrupt generation."

Brentano (1778–1842)

Like his friend Görres, Clemens Brentano only returned to the Catholic faith of his childhood after following all kinds of false paths. Otherwise the two great Rhinelanders were very different. The undisciplined imagination and overflowing genius of Brentano were in strong contrast to the firm steadiness of

Görres. The lack of unified education and firm discipline affected both his character and his art. His works are the chance products of a life which was aimless but determined by poetic and religious motives.

Ina Seidel has described Brentano as the purest lyric poet in German literature. Even his prose is lyrical. His style is musical and flowing; it aims above all at producing harmonious sounds and is therefore the reverse of plastic and precise. His thought, feelings and actions all lack decision. Complaints at the dichotomy in his mind and nostalgia for God are frequent themes in the work of his early period. "This never-ending struggle with himself was the real story of his life and literary work" (Eichendorff). The *Chronicles of a Travelling Scholar* betrays his longing for simplicity and homely faith, while the *Romances of the Rosary* reflect the writer's false steps: sin and virtue struggle with one another in this unfinished epic poem which has been called "the Catholic Faust". The *Romances of the Rosary* rank beside Annette von Droste-Hülshoff's *Spiritual Year* as "the profoundest mystical expression of Catholic devotion" (Richard von Schaukal).

Under the influence of Sailer, the gifted Catholic educationist, and of the Protestant clergyman's daughter Luise Henkel, author of the hymn *Müde bin ich, geh zur Ruh* ("I am tired and go to rest"), Brentano found the faith again. Testimony to his conversion is the poem *Spring-cry of a Servant from the Depths*.

Lord, have pity on me, that my heart may bloom afresh!

Another poem that dates from the period of inner struggle and conversion is the one entitled *To the Angel in the Wilderness*:

I fell into despair, because I found no water. . . .
Then I saw the angel of the wilderness with his dewy wings . . . .

"Tell me, angel of the wilderness,
Where can I find the spring of water?" He replied:
"He who truly repents stands at the fountain's brink" . . .

Silently I knelt before him; he laid his cool and dewy feathers round my glowing head, and sang to me pilgrim's songs.
I loved and believed.

The last line reminds us of Chateaubriand's "I wept and believed." Among the many things which Chateaubriand and Brentano have in common is an emotional religiosity.

While enjoyment and devouring longing are the basic themes of the poetry written before his conversion, in his later lyrics, which are almost exclusively religious, an entirely new note is heard, a note of child-like, heartfelt sincerity. Brentano is no longer a prey to gnawing introspection; he has found peace. Just as earlier he surrendered himself to his wild imagination, so now he surrenders himself to his faith.

Brentano spent five years at the bedside of the stigmatic Anna Katharina Emmerich at Dülmen, and wrote down her visions. These journals appeared in an adapted form under the titles *The Bitter Suffering of Our Lord and Saviour Jesus Christ*, *The Life of the Virgin Mary* and *The Life of Our Lord and Saviour Jesus Christ*. They went through innumerable editions, were translated into many languages and have nourished Christian piety until the present day.

Eichendorff (1788–1857)

"Eichendorff is too often dismissed by superficial critics as the naïve, contented wanderer who 'leaves everything to God' . . . Eichendorff is familiar with life's riddles and problems. He struggles with them, but with the confidence born of faith, that is sure of final victory" (Köhler). The poet tells us how profoundly he was affected in his childhood by the encounter with our Lord's passion: "I cannot describe in words what I felt. I wept from the bottom of my heart, so much so that I sobbed. My whole being was filled and permeated with it." He goes on to say that this experience permanently altered his life. From then onward, for him the cross was a symbol of unparalleled suffering and painful riddles, but at the same time a symbol of redemption and of the victory over death and the devil. The gaiety of Eichendorff's poetry, its unalloyed joy and child-like trust spring from his experience of the cross, and when the poet sings "I leave everything to God" it is no prettification of the world and God, but a victory over the sorrow of the world and a conquest of despair through faith. "When all around him falls", the poet opens himself to the power from above: "Therefore God has given him the word that boldly names the darkest things, a pious earnestness amid life's riches, the joy that no one else knows."

This attitude differentiates Eichendorff from many other Romantic writers, who either avoided the difficulties of life or gave way to despair. Like a Christian knight, he looked reality bravely in the face and dared to swim against the stream. "Eichendorff never followed a fashion", said Hermann Hesse, and the remark is true not only of his art but also of his mental attitude. With his faculties wide awake he lived through the shattering changes which the period between the French Revolution and the revolution of 1848 brought with it:

> The reign of faith is over, the old splendour
> Has been destroyed,
> Beauty has been turned away in tears,
> So graceless is our age.

In this situation a man like Eichendorff was bound to win the reputation of being a narrow-minded reactionary, although in reality he saw further into the future than most of his contemporaries, fought all through his life against the Philistines, and would have nothing to do with the "prudery of mawkish Pietists":

> When a man still holds the Standard of Christ above earthly rubbish, the world considers him a fool and a fabulous wonder.

Eichendorff was a born fighter. When the Prussian government had the Archbishop of Cologne arrested, Eichendorff openly criticized their action, took up his stand by the side of Görres, and resigned his post in the Prussian Ministry of Internal Affairs. The struggles between Church and State that characterized the period are also reflected in his poetry, and not in satirical or polemical form alone. He sees the approaching storms, the flashes of lightning, the "breakers" rolling in, the yawning "abyss", and "a secret horror" creeps over him. But he prays:

> Thy will, O Lord, be done!
> The land is dark and silent,
> And in the approaching storm
> I recognize with a shudder thy hand.

In one of his poems, he sees, in the midst of the stormy waves and the uproar of the elements, "the ship of the Church" quietly and surely proceeding on its way. In another, he trusts, amid the storms of the time, to the Lord of History. A third poem is a summons to awake: "For the Lord wishes to hold a review in German lands, and to count those who have remained true to him, before he sends the angel with the sword. Already there is a dull red gleam in the grey of dawn; whether it signifies blood or fiery love depends on God, whose hand no one can avert."

The Lord goes the rounds and seeks his own, but finds the doors shut everywhere. The poet makes himself God's herald:

> On gates of palace and cottage alike will I knock.
> Up! Already the peaks are ablaze, wake up, wake up!

Shortly before his death he wrote these lines: "The world falls into horrid ruin, but one thing, overlooked in haste, remains standing alone on the ruins: the Cross. The hero, tired from toil, sinks on his knee before the image which will redeem all of us, lays down his blood-stained weapons and leaves his free sons to build afresh."

Just as Eichendorff was far removed from middle-class complacency in his view of the age in which he lived, so his picture of nature is by no means idyllic. Even the gentler scenes are surrounded by storms. He, too, had certainly been captivated by the spell of nature, but he rose superior to it. "If nature beckons with wild delight", it must be resisted, for nature is an "abyss" like the human heart, full of demoniac powers. He is forewarned against the toils of "earthly delight and magic": "Prayer always triumphs over magic and rises victoriously to heaven." Eichendorff's whole spiritual development and devotional attitude is summed up in one of the *Spiritual Poems* which bears the inscription *The Boatman*. The first stanza conjures up the legendary dream-world and nature-magic of Romanticism, the second destroys the illusion. For the images of Nature are not the ultimate reality, but only symbols of the ultimate reality. The poet cannot settle down in this world; he longs for eternal reality: "I shall walk through this world, with its misery and joy, as a happy pilgrim, and use it only as a bridge to thee, Lord, across the stream of time."

That is the basic attitude behind the *Spiritual Poems*. The titles of the individual poems in the collection indicate the images in which the poet portrays symbolically his relationship to the world and to God: *The Boatman, The Soldier, The Watchman, The Return, The Sick Man, The Pilgrim, The Pilot, The Hermit, The Singer*. The conclusion, whether explicit or implicit, is always "Onward!" and "Upward!" Eichendorff struggles on toward God,

As a buried miner digs himself out to the fresh air.

Eichendorff is a truly Catholic poet, not simply by virtue of his *Spiritual Poems* or of his *Song of Mary*, which was written at the instigation of his friend the Bishop of Ermland, incorporated in the diocesan hymn-book and often sung; or by virtue of *Lucius*, the youthful story of an early Christian martyr; or even of the *Life of St Hedwig,* which he began at the request of his other episcopal friend, the Prince-Bishop Förster of Breslau. He is Catholic in everything he wrote, for even the poems and stories on non-religious subjects are the product of the same devoutness as the works with religious themes. Christianity permeates Eichendorff's whole work, in accordance with his own demand as a critic: "We ask for nothing but a Christian atmosphere, which we breathe unconsciously, and which, in its purity, allows the hidden higher meaning of earthly things to shine through of its own accord." Since, as a writer, he himself fulfilled this demand, he performed the religious mission which he attributed to all literature.

In his critical works (*On the Ethical and Religious Signifi-cance of Modern Romantic Poetry in Germany*; *Religious Poetry in Germany*; *The German Novel of the Eighteenth Century in Relation to Christianity*; *History of the Drama*), Eichendorff estimated the value of individual works according to the degree in which they fulfil the religious task of literature. This procedure can be criticized on the grounds that literature cannot be measured by non-literary standards. It is certainly true that only literary standards can determine what is litera-ture and what is not. Yet the great modern poet and critic T. S. Eliot maintains that it is "necessary to measure literature by clear ethical and theological standards. The greatness of literature cannot be determined by literary standards alone." Therein lies a justification of the critical method of Eichen-dorff, who judged literature from a Catholic standpoint. That the width of his horizon did not suffer as a result is shown by his warm appreciation of non-Catholic but genuinely Christian writers like Luther and Arnim.[1] As the Protestant critic Grol-man pointed out, Eichendorff dared to adopt a denominational standpoint without limiting his outlook.

"In Eichendorff Romantic longing receives its most unequi-vocally Christian stamp. With him, all wandering and longing is directed towards a clear, supernatural goal" (Hankamer). And Eichendorff's Christian optimism regards this goal as attainable, in contrast to Schiller whose *Pilgrim* ends in tired resignation:

> Alas, no path leads there, heaven above me will never touch the earth, and "there" is never "here".

The hero of Eichendorff's best story, *The Good-for-nothing*, is the wanderer in the adventure of life. He has nothing to fall back on, but he has a sense of mystery, and in the end every-thing turns out all right for him, for he reaches the goal of his

[1] Achim von Arnim (1781–1831) was another prominent German Romantic writer. He collaborated with Brentano in editing the famous collection of folk-songs *Des Knaben Wunderhorn* (1806–8) and married Brentano's sister. (*Trans.*)

longing. It is not by chance that the word "homeward" is always recurring in Eichendorff's work. One of the sources of his poetry is his love of home, his heartfelt devotion to the castle of Lubowitz and its woods in Silesia. When this ancestral home was lost, it assumed in the poet's memory a particular radiance as a symbol of our home in heaven.

To return there after long travels abroad was for Eichendorff throughout his life the fulfilment of his longing. This idea receives particularly strong and gripping expression in the eighth poem of the series *On the Death of my Child*. The poet sits at home with his family in the lamplight and listens to the stormy night outside. He thinks of his dead child: "It seems as if you were bound to knock gently at the door, as if you had only lost your way and were now returning tired."

The mood of oppression is suddenly lit up by the realization that the conception on which it is based is false: "Poor fools that we are!" In reality the situation is the reverse of what it was thought to be:

> It is we who wander in fear, still lost in the dark—
> You reached home long ago.

Annette von Droste-Hülshoff (1797–1848)

Reinhold Schneider considered that no German writer of the nineteenth century was so far up "in the forefront of the spiritual struggle" as Annette von Droste-Hülshoff, "with her penetrating intellect and proud, chivalrous heart." The physically delicate aristocrat from Münster was a "masculine poetess" (Mary Lavater-Sloman). "Her faith lives, like all living faith since the Middle Ages, on the alternation between emotion and coldness, exaltation and fear" (Kurt Hohoff). "Into the soul, believing and wishing to believe, press the doubting voices of the future. . . . In imagery drawn from the mysterious, hidden forces of nature and the ghostly visions of Westphalian folklore, her poetry hints at a world partly controlled by demoniac powers" (Gertrud von le Fort).

This becomes particularly clear in the poem *The Familiar*

Spirit of the Horse-dealer, which can be described either as a long ballad or as a short epic. It has been described as "her most powerful work . . . the climax of the German ballad" (Heselhaus), "an unparalleled masterpiece" (Reinhold Schneider). The theme is the problem of evil in the world and the defeat of magic by faith and love. The unfortunate horse-dealer, who sold his soul to the devil for wealth, power and reputation, can in the end only be saved by the cross.

Annette gave testimony of her own lonely struggle in her *Spiritual Year.* In the preface to this book she explains that it is not written "for all devout people . . . a temperament inclined to simple, child-like piety would not even understand it. It is for the secret, but certainly widespread, band of those whose love is greater than their faith, for those unhappy but foolish people who ask more questions in an hour than seven wise men could answer in seven years." The *Spiritual Year* is a cycle of contemplations and prayers in verse. The author uses the Gospels of the Sundays and feast-days of the liturgical year as starting-points, but applies the word of God directly to her own situation. Yet in spite of their personal colouring these poems can claim universal validity, for in the author's need is expressed the need of modern man in general.

She sees herself as "a child shut out", "the beggar barred outside the gates":

> Ich muss in grossen Peinen
> Einsam liegen vor der Tür[2]

waiting for a crumb from the table of the Lord like the little dog with which Christ compares the Canaanite woman. How often has she "cried out in the darkness" with "night's horror all around her." She runs like "the wounded stag" without finding the way; if the wolf does not devour her, she will sink in the marsh. She is already "half-drowned":

> All confused, I know not where to turn;
> the ground heaves threateningly all round me.

[2] I have to lie in misery
alone outside the door.

She knows the condition of her soul, "how lacking in faith, how defiant and confused" it is. She seeks something "to carry her over the abyss." But doubts prevent her seeing what can save her:

> He who believes will receive salvation;
> but what of him whom life has robbed, in hidden pains,
> of his treasure?

Her quest remains unsuccessful:

> See, I have sought thee, my Lord and God, with sorrow;
> where shall I find thee? Not in my own dead heart,
> where sin long since effaced thine image.

She can only fold her hands in the darkness:

> Alas, the wilderness is not beside me;
> it lies in my own bosom!

Nietzsche was to say later on:

> The wilderness grows!
> Woe to him, who hides a wilderness within him!

And poets like T. S. Eliot and Ernst Jünger were to use the wasteland as a symbol of nihilism. Annette compares herself to the Jewish people: "Thus Israel wandered for forty years, and sought and sought, and found a grave of wilderness."

He who reaches the Promised Land after long wandering in the wilderness knows how to value it better than some one who always lived in it: "Oh, only he who stood in the blazing desert can appreciate the value of a green leaf."

Annette has already experienced existential nihilism:

> I am destroyed,
> I am annihilated,
> And slowly turning away
> My glance rests on nothingness.

Faith bursts forth all the more powerfully, first only a tiny seed, but full of unconquerable life:

> In the curse, at which all shudder, thou canst hear the complaint, broken in strength and courage; in the criminal's madness

there is the beating of a lacerated heart. That is the seed, which, as though in a dream, bores anxiously with its roots into the ground, and always bears the green of life within it, a tree still slumbering. Break into my heart, O Lord, thou knowest how to push. . . . [It is not despair that has the last word, but trusting faith:]
If sorrow devours me, and I lose what is dearest to me; if I feel no comfort, and no prayer of mine is heard, it can only lead me to thee; so be welcome, flame and sword!

Here (as also in the deeply moving poems *The Groaning Creature* and *Gethsemane*) Annette experiences the mysticism of suffering. As Heselhaus says, "The union with God, which she is unable to attain with the confidence born of joy, is revealed to her in the abyss of suffering. The last poems of this cycle are among the most profound products of the nineteenth century in the field of the religious lyric and in that of religious art in general. . . . The *Spiritual Year* is genuine poetry, a noble work whose sharp dichotomy and density of thought make it deeply affecting." R. A. Schröder has called it Annette's "central and decisive work." Those who know it are unanimous in the view that it has no parallel in German religious literature of the nineteenth century.

From an artistic point of view, Annette only surpassed the *Spiritual Year* in *Gethsemane*. Here the severity of the language is suited to the dreadful seriousness of the subject. Even the physical aspect of the outbreak of sweat is vividly brought out. The trembling Christ sees in a vision his body stretched out on the cross; he sees the sinews standing out on his limbs like cords, the blood dripping from the crown of thorns and the head lolling to and fro in the death agony. Nature around him is distorted in suffering as he is. As Hagelstange puts it, "Annette von Droste-Hülshoff provided in this poem a great example of Christian poetry; and the 'Christian' is not to be understood (as often) as indicating an artistic limitation, but simply as a descriptive adjective. She provided an example of great poetry."

NATURE MYSTICISM

Gezelle (1830–99)

This son of a Bruges nursery-gardener, who became a priest and a poet, remained relatively unknown during his lifetime, which was full of sorrow. His restrained lyrics were completely overlooked by his contemporaries. That Gezelle wrote in old Flemish was one of the reasons that at first prevented his work from achieving a wider reputation. These homely poems, the products of profound piety and of Gezelle's love for his native West Flanders, were only discovered and praised by the Dutch modernists. German readers were introduced to them by Rudolf Alexander Schröder, who rates individual poems of Gezelle above the work of Verlaine and Rimbaud.

Gezelle's religious poems are informed by a quiet, heartfelt trust in God. In Gezelle, faith is as self-evident as his love of nature. The finest nuances of nature are all reflected in his work; sound, colour and form are all rendered with the greatest accuracy. But the poet's perception goes beyond the purely sensuous.

The material content only provides the starting-point; it is transformed and spiritualized into something more mysterious. The result is a lyricism that is at the same time both spiritual and earthly. A good example is the poem *Ego Flos,* which includes the following lines:

> Let me see thine infinite light in the heavenly home.
> Then shall I stand and blossom, not before thine eyes, but near thee, beside thee, in thee, where thou let'st thy poor creature absorb fullness of life, where thou let'st me enter thine eternal light.

"The recognition of God's infinity in his finite creation by means of a direct act of perception lends Gezelle's poetry the character of a mystical vision" (Hechtle). The reader is reminded of the great Flemish mystic Ruysbroeck, and also of the Flemish priest-poet Cyriel Verschaeve, who carried on Gezelle's manner.

Gezelle's *Churchyard Flowers* portray, sometimes in controlled, at others in uncontrolled language, the burial of one of the poet's friends and disciples. Over all human misery hovers the cheerfulness of a devout temperament. Sublime simplicity here becomes sublime art.

One of Gezelle's loveliest *Spiritual Poems* is *O Grain of Incense*. "In it meet, as though in a burning glass, all the rays of his being, earthly misery and the sigh of the ephemeral creature and, in contrast to these, shimmering confidence and certainty of eternity, expressed in the symbol of the grain of incense offered up in sacrifice:"

> Tear of larch and cedar,
> Image of prayer,
> In which fire plays
> And sparks from the heart's flame!

Flowers, trees, sun, moon, animals, birds, and their relations to their Creator, together with friendship—these are the themes of this tender poet. He holds conversations with trees and birds, and learns from them about the universal creator.

"A gaiety in God that reminds us of St Francis of Assisi is here expressed, that on occasion—even if very seldom—rises to humour" (Hechtle). But melancholy moods are more characteristic of Gezelle:

> Let the song that rustles in the slender reed echo in my sad song, and with its complaint reach thee, who gavest life to it and me; O thou who art pleased by the lament the reed-stalk sings thee, be content also with my plaintive song, for I, too, am a poor, sick, mourning reed!

Gerard Manley Hopkins (1844–89)

Hopkins cannot be identified with any school or any theory. He is an erratic boulder in the landscape of European literature: he sticks out, but his origins remain unknown. It has been said of Hopkins that he appeared on the poetic scene by a sort of virgin birth. It is certainly difficult to name a spiritual progenitor. Right from the start he displayed such stubborn originality that even Robert Bridges, his friend and editor, spoke of "violence", "obscurity" and "curiosities". Hopkins was a revolutionary. His bold originality shattered inherited forms of expression, melted them down into new possibilities and forged them into unusual shapes. Worn literary coins he stamped out afresh and endowed with a new brilliance. He either gave the words he used new meanings, or else awoke in them a meaning that until then had been slumbering. By so doing he gave them new, vigorous life but at the same time made comprehension difficult. "Of Hopkins least of all can it be said that the English literary language thinks and writes for him; rather does he write and think for the English language, extending its frontiers in all directions" (Irene Behn). It is no wonder that when he was discovered, after the First World War, he made disciples in all the Anglo-Saxon countries, and in France, Holland and Italy as well. He exercised a decisive influence on W. H. Auden and Dylan Thomas.

In his prosody, Hopkins forged classical, native and personal forms into something new. His "sprung rhythm" returns to the Germanic principle of accentuation. This kind of line moulds itself completely to the poet's will. It can storm the reader's ear with breath-taking power, it can flow merrily along in gentle waves, and it can simulate the violent blows of a whip. These effects are intensified, but at the same time also con-trolled, by alliteration. In Hopkins' poetry, alliteration comes into its own again as a means of expression of unparalleled dynamism. Hopkins achieved a still more striking effect by giving preference to vigorous, monosyllabic Anglo-Saxon words, avoiding expletives, and even omitting constructive elements like relative pronouns. He also altered the conven-tional word-order, and was thus able to give particularly strong emphasis to individual words. Pressed together like this, the colours shine with a metallic gleam. And by binding the vowels together in assonances, end-rhymes and internal rhymes, Hopkins created a very effective verbal music.

This poetry is taut with original wildness. Again and again

Hopkins praises wilderness and wild-flowers, water and wind. He had the Germanic urge for the boundless, the infinite. But at the same time his heart was full of the Greek love of rounded beauty, perfected form. His nature is a mixture of elemental sensuality and ascetic discipline. He was capable of the most extraordinary stoppages. When Hopkins, who was received into the Church by Newman, entered the Society of Jesus he renounced writing. For seven years he was silent, until he was commissioned by his superiors to sing the fate of the five Franciscan nuns who were drowned on the high seas fleeing from Germany as a result of the *Kulturkampf*, the Prussian government's dispute with Rome. Then the barrage gave way and the dammed-up forces broke loose. The result was the creation of his most powerful poem, *The Wreck of the Deutschland,* and all his best sonnets. In fourteen years the greatest poems of the age were written. They are poems of wild yet precisely controlled beauty. They give the impression of a joyous shout of freedom, yet at the same time the reader senses that the forces set free are also disciplined. The poet likes to use the strict form of the sonnet. The following sonnet will give some idea how he piles up cyclopian blocks of language on a narrow foundation, how he ascends from the depths of chaos to a lofty order, how he subordinates all linguistic means to this ascent and combines them in an orchestral body of sound:

> The world is charged with the grandeur of God.
>   It will flame out, like shining from shook foil;
>   It gathers to a greatness, like the ooze of oil
> Crushed. Why do men then now not reck his rod?
> Generations have trod, have trod, have trod;
>   And all is seared with trade; bleared, smeared with toil:
>   And wears man's smudge and shares man's smell; the soil
>   Is base now, nor can foot feel, being shod.
>
> And for all this, nature is never spent;
>   There lives the dearest freshness deep down things;
> And though the last lights off the black West went

Oh, Morning, at the brown brink eastward, springs—
Because the Holy Ghost over the bent
World broods with warm breast and with oh! bright wings.

"Nor can foot feel, being shod." For the poet, it was a real
pleasure to walk over the earth with bare feet. In the *Epithalamion* he cannot pull his shoes off quick enough, "till walk the
world he can with bare his feet". But in the industrial age, man
no longer has any direct contact with the ground, with nature,
with Mother earth. Hard-shod feet symbolize this. The thought
recurs in *Tom's Garland*. The poet himself explains in a letter
which mentions this poem: "The foot is the day-labourer, and
this is armed with hobnail boots, because it has to wear and
be worn by the ground; which again is symbolical, for it is
navvies or day-labourers who, on the great scale or in gangs
and millions, mainly trench, tunnel, blast, and in other ways
disfigure, 'mammock' the earth and, on a small scale, singly
and superficially stamp it with their footprints." But *natura
naturans*, that is "never spent", triumphs over man's work
that consumes and besmirches the ground. In this force, "the
dearest freshness deep down things", Hopkins sees the Holy
Ghost himself. The last lines agree with Basilius' commentary
on the biblical account of the creation: "The spirit of God
moved over the waters. . . . The word 'moved' is taken in the
sense of 'warmed'. The Holy Spirit made the nature of the
water life-giving; in the same way as a broody bird warms the
eggs and endows them with a sort of life-giving force. This is
the meaning that lies in the words 'the spirit moved', that is,
it affected the nature of the water so that it brought forth
living creatures." That is Hopkins' aim: to show that nature
rests in God and lives from God. The creation proclaims the
Creator, and because the poet loves the Creator he also loves
his creatures. They all praise God, and to praise God is the
poet's task.

He loves the call of the cuckoo, which opens up the springs
of ear and heart and makes the whole land suddenly blossom
out; the trilling song of the skylark that climbs longingly in the

sunlight and sinks down in happiness; the morning's favourite, the crown-prince of the realm of day, the falcon soaring steeply upward on the breeze; the crinkly, silky, bright red poppy, whose petals are like blood or fire; the poplars, whose airy tops muffle the blazing sun; the dark mountain-stream that bubbles down its rocky road like a brown horse's back; the curves of the hills; the night, the moon and the stars; the storm; the sea; weeds and wilderness. He praises the Lord, who created, gives life to, unites and upholds this multifarious and often contradictory variety:

> Glory be to God for dappled things—
>   For skies of couple-colour as a brinded cow;
>   For rose-moles all in stipple upon trout that swim:
> Fresh-firecoal chestnut-falls; finches' wings;
>   Landscape plotted and pieced-fold, fallow, and plough;
>   And áll trádes, their gear and tackle and trim.
>
> All things counter, original, spare, strange;
>   Whatever is fickle, freckled (who knows how?)
>   With swift, slow; sweet, sour; adazzle, dim;
> He fathers-forth whose beauty is past change:
>   Praise him.

From admiration of creatures the poet is carried on to adoring admiration of the Creator, from animal energy, which is always trying to expand its empire in all directions, to spiritual love, which is focused on God alone. As he returns from fishing, he is aware of his Redeemer in the landscape:

> And the azurous hung hills are his world-wielding shoulder
> Majestic—as a stallion stalwart, very-violet-sweet!

Spring makes the poet rejoice, but it also makes the spiritual adviser worry about youthful innocence, which is so easily lost:

> Nothing is so beautiful as spring—
>   When weeds, in wheels, shoot long and lovely and lush;
>   Thrush's eggs look little low heavens, and thrush
> Through the echoing timber does so rinse and wring
> The ear, it strikes like lightnings to hear him sing;

The glassy peartree leaves and blooms, they brush
The descending blue; that blue is all in a rush
With richness; the racing lambs too have fair their fling.
What is all this juice and joy?
A strain of the earth's sweet being in the beginning
In Eden garden.—Have, get, before it cloy,
Before it cloud, Christ, lord, and sour with sinning,
Innocent mind and Mayday in girl and boy,
Most, O maid's child, thy choice and worthy the winning.

The poet loves man in nature: boys bathing boisterously and noisily in the river, "with dare and with downdolphinry and bell-bright bodies huddling out", in the shade of beech and ash trees; Harry the ploughman, with his "hard as hurdle arms, with a broth of goldish hue/Breathed round", "barrelled shank", watchful eyes, sinewy, firm, with a charm of his own, bent over the plough; Tom the day-labourer, on his way home with his pick on his shoulder; Felix Randal, the sturdy farrier. The nobility of nature is united with the nobility of man redeemed. Every being shows forth in its activity the Creator, its model: "Christ plays in a thousand places, plays charmingly in limbs and eyes that are not his own, plays before the Father in the faces of men".

Original, undiluted sensuality reveals the holy. In his *Epithalamion* Hopkins compares the sacrament of marriage to a lush, wooded valley with a river tumbling through it. The water is married love. Man pulls off his boots and clothes in happy, excited haste, runs bare-footed over the ground to the beautifully fresh water, lets the friendly waves lap his limbs, looks round happily, laughs and swims. In a hymn, he compares the Virgin Mary to the air we breathe. Just as the world-mothering atmosphere is the essential element of life for everything, so Mary as Mother passes on to us the graces of the supernatural life. And just as the blue atmosphere filters the light of the sun, which would otherwise dazzle us, so Mary, as Mother of God, gives to humanity in visible shape what would otherwise have to remain invisible.

Hopkins, who composed and played music, drew and painted, possessed a highly developed sense of beauty. He was also vividly aware how ephemeral it was. Again and again he was overcome by sorrow at the fragility of nature. The Binsey poplars are "all felled, felled, are all felled", and the poet breaks out into the lament: "O if we but knew what we do / when we delve or hew— / Hack and rack the growing green!" Like Cowper and Thompson, Hopkins feels before felled trees: "Since country is so tender / To touch, her being só slender, / That, like this sleek and seeing ball / But a pick will make no eye at all, / Where we, even where we mean / To mend her we end her, / When we hew or delve: / After-comers cannot guess the beauty been." Before the portrait of two beautiful young people he says:

> O I admire and sorrow! The heart's eye grieves
> Discovering you, dark tramplers, tyrant years.
> A juice rides rich through bluebells, in vine leaves,
> And beauty's dearest veriest vein is tears.

Hopkins knows the reason for this grief. He tells little Margaret, who is upset because the wood is losing its leaves: the source of all grief is one and the same: man's hereditary curse. Hopkins also knows the consolation: Nature is a Heraclitean fire which is continually renewed, and man is destined to rise again. In St Winefred's Well, the Leaden Echo calls out in despair: "How to keep / Back Beauty, keep it . . . from vanishing away." But the Golden Echo replies: "Give beauty back . . . to God, beauty's self and beauty's giver." These lines remind us both to accept things gratefully and to sacrifice them readily.

The freedom of the human will can also destroy the beauty of the soul. "The best becomes the worst. What worm was here, gnawing away wood reaching for heaven?" The filth and misery of the slums of Liverpool and Dublin moved Hopkins the priest deeply. This, too, entered into his poetry; we find laments for lost purity of soul, warnings to purity still preserved. He feels for society's outcasts, the "unemployed, beggars, tramps, street loafers, the despairing, the apathetic, radical socialists, werewolves and gallows-birds, the rabble that infects the age." The poem *The Bugler's First Communion* gives us a glimpse of his heart struggling with God between fear and hope for a human soul. But the most personal poems are those "dreadful sonnets", in which he is locked in combat with God for himself. This mystic, whom the mere reflection of divine beauty aroused to ecstatic jubilation, also knew "the dark night of the soul," in which cries of pain echo in the distance far away from God:

I wake and feel the fell of dark, not day.
What hours, O what black hours we have spent
This night! What sighs you, heart, saw; ways you went!
And more must, in yet longer light's delay.
  With witness I speak this. But when I say
Hours I mean years, mean life. And my lament
Is cries countless, cries like dead letters sent
To dearest him that lives alas! away.
  I am gall, I am heartburn. God's most deep decree
Bitter would have me taste: my taste was me;
Bones built in me, flesh filled, blood brimmed the curse,
  Selfyeast of spirit a dull dough sours. I see
The lost are like this, and their scourge to be
As I am mine, their sweating selves, but worse.

This is a mysterious realm, which remains closed to most men. Modern man can perhaps sense the abyss, but can he believe that this abyss is blessed? Hopkins knew that it was. He is in the tradition of St John of the Cross. But even from this dark region echo words in which every man finds his own troubles reflected. A good example is the sonnet which, bridging millenia, begins with the complaint of Jeremias:

Thou art indeed just, Lord, if I contend
With thee; but, sir, so what I plead is just.
Why do sinner's ways prosper? and why must
Disappointment all I endeavour end?

Wert thou my enemy, O thou my friend,
How wouldst thou worse, I wonder, than thou dost
Defeat, thwart me? Oh, the sots and thralls of lust
Do in spare hours more thrive than I that spend,
Sir, life upon thy cause. See, banks and brakes
Now, leaved how thick! laced they are again
With pretty chervil, look, and fresh wind shakes
Them; birds build—but not I build; no, but strain,
Time's eunuch, and not breed one work that wakes.
Mine, O thou lord of life, send my roots rain.

Francis Thompson (1857–1907)

Swinburne said that the pale Galilean had not been able to win the laurel, the palm or the paean. Francis Thompson retorted that the Church had once been the Mother not only of the saints but also of the poets. It could not be denied, however, that poetry had long ceased to be a faithful daughter of the Church. More effective evidence of Thompson's claim was required, and this, too, he provided in his own poetic work. He outlined his aims in these words: "It is something to be the poet of the return to nature; but I should like to be the poet of the return to God."

He had to wear the crown of thorns before the laurel adorned his temples. His poetry springs from a soul filled with sorrow. For Thompson, pain was the "icy bath that doth string the slack sinews loosened with happiness", the great guardian and protector of God's treasures, the "portress in the gateways of all love". Sorrow shows the way to the gifts of wisdom and polishes the poet's tarnished crown so that it shines more brightly. It is the oil of suffering that consecrates the poet.

In his misery Thompson experienced the insufficiency of the human and the transitory nature of earthly things. The felled yew-tree wakes in his soul a throng of echoing pictures of mortality. He is filled with grief by the thought that the sun never sets in the same way twice. Flowers are never again the flowers of yesterday evening. The first kiss cannot be repeated. Of all the empty words that fall from man's mouth, none is so empty as "once more" and "again". For there is no second joy. There is just one at the beginning, and then it is past: through the whole of life we are continually walking away from it and looking back at it. This consciousness of the pitiless tyranny of time over all created things is at the bottom of all Thompson's poems. Not that he has never rejoiced in the creation; dull melancholy does not cloud all his work. He is perfectly capable of adopting a cheerful tone. Those jubilant spring roundelays, the *Sister Songs*, are full of the scent of flowers, heavenly music and great joy. The *Children's Poems* contain pictures which remind us of paradise. A reflection of bliss shimmers through these verses, but only a reflection, not bliss itself. Here, too, the poet senses "the sadness in the sweet, the sweetness in the sad": "The fairest things have fleetest end . . . Nothing begins, nothing ends, that is not paid with moan. For we are born in other's pain and perish in our own."

Nature, although transitory, is beautiful. And Thompson, who always felt that he was "a hermit of beauty, girded around with a thirsty loneliness of soul", found the creation glorious, for it is a copy of the glory of its creator. His song is celebration, adoration, praise and thanks; but it is also the complaint, the sighing of the creature. For nature, although beautiful, is transitory; and the creation is only a copy, not the actual glory, of the creator. The poet praises the creator for his most beautiful creation:

> A perfect woman—Thine be laud!
> Her body is a temple of God.

And he "loves the beauty of his house".

Lovingly he portrays the woman whom the man in him calls "beloved", the child in him "mother". The charm of her body is so much the expression of her soul that he can stop contemplating the immortal whose every feature is implied by the mortal. God laid his finger on the ivory of her pure limbs as though on gentle keys and breathed out there her spirit's harmonies.

Yet here too the inadequacy of the human becomes evident; this time it is the inadequacy of language:

> Now all is said, but woe is me!—
> Her real self remains unexpressed.

He wishes that we still had the tongue in which Adam spoke with God in paradise; our uncontrolled speech is a legacy from the masons of Babel. It is beyond its power to capture the highest beauty. So Thompson's love of beauty is an unhappy love: he knows that he has fallen a victim to beauty, that he is hers for ever, and that she will never be his. He is fully conscious of his "possible affinity with mud". Full of longing, he glimpses the dead Cardinal of Westminster in the joy of heaven: "But I, ex-Paradised, the shoulder of your Christ find high to lean thereby, so flaps my helpless sail" filled neither by the wind of heaven nor by that of hell. Life is a piece of coquetry by death, which soon tires me, for I am too certain of the love; a wardrobe, in which I try on various garments of death, until I find a fashion that suits me. As a Christian, he is certain that there is such a thing as eternal happiness, but by no means certain that he will share in it. This uncertainty is expressed with particular urgency in the sonnet *Non Pax-Expectatio*:

> Hush! 'tis the gap between two lightnings. Room
> Is none for peace in this thou callest peace,
> This breathing-while wherein the breathings cease.
> The pulses sicken, hearkening through the gloom.
> Afar the thunders of a coming doom
> Ramp on the cowering winds. Lo! at the dread,
> Thy heart's tomb yawns and renders up its dead,—
> The hopes 'gainst hope embalmed in its womb.
>
> Canst thou endure, if the pent flood o'erflows?
> Who is estated heir to constancy?
> Behold, I hardly know if I outlast
> The minute underneath whose heel I lie;
> Yet I endure, have stayed the minute passed,
> Perchance may stay the next. Who knows, who knows?

All the things that fill Thompson with sadness—the transitory nature of the creation, the inconstancy of things, the uncertainty of human life—are summed up in the poem *Absence*:

> When music's fading's faded,
>   And the rose's death is dead,
> And my heart is fain of tears, because
>   Mine eyes have none to shed;
>   I said,
>   Whence shall faith be fed?
>
> Canst thou be what thou hast been?
>   No, no more what thou hast!
> Lo, all last things that I have known,
>   And all that shall be last,
>   Went past
>   With the thing thou wast!
>
> If the petal of this Spring be
>   As of the Spring that's flown,
> If the thought that now as sweet is
>   As the sweet thought overblown;
>   Alone
>   Canst thou be thyself gone.
>
> To yester-rose a richer
>   The rose-spray may bear;
> Thrice thousand fairer you may be,—
>   But tears for the fair
>   You were
>   When you first were fair!
>
> .   .   .   .
>
> Sweet shall have its sorrow,
>   The rainbow its rain,
> Loving have its leaving,
>   And bliss is of pain
>   So fain,
>   Ah, is she bliss or pain?

In this bottomless sadness Thompson resembles the Shelley whom he revered so much and on whom he wrote his best essay. But the differences between the two poets should not be overlooked. Thompson says what Shelley would never have dared to say: "Look, here Nature and I stand face to face, and I am the greater. Bend down at my feet, thou who art poor in heart, fair in gesture, strong in weak purposes, lovely beast of prey. I am not one of the fools who call thee goddess."

> O heart of Nature! did man ever hear
> Thy yearned-for word, supposèd dear?—
> His pleading voice returns to him alone;
> He hears none other tone.
> No, no;
> Take back, O poets, your praises little-wise,
> Nor fool weak hearts to their unskinned distress,
> Who deem that even after your device
> They shall lie down in Nature's holiness:
> For it was never so;
> She has no hands to bless us
> . . . .
> O man, she has no use, nor asks not, for thy knee,
> . . . .
> If thou wouldst bend in prayer,
> Arise, pass forth; thou must look otherwhere.

But in the same poem he addresses nature as "Lady divine". He explains that this woman is God's daughter, but she only gives her hand to his friends, her Father's friends. Shelley could not have said that either. What Thompson means here is explained in his essay *Nature's Immortality:*

> You go to . . . Nature, and you look for—sympathy? Yes; the sympathy of a cat, sitting by the fire and blinking at you. . . . She knows that she is beautiful, and she is placidly content with the knowledge; she was made to be gazed on, and she fulfils the end of her creation. . . . What is this heart of Nature, if it exist at all? Is it, according to the conventional doctrine derived from Wordsworth and Shelley, a heart of love, according with the heart of man, and stealing out to him through a thousand avenues of mute sympathy? No; in this sense I repeat seriously what I said lightly: Nature has no heart. . . . Absolute nature

lives not in our life, nor yet is lifeless, but lives in the life of God: and in so far, and so far merely, as man himself lives in that life, does he come into sympathy with Nature, and Nature with him. She is God's daughter, who stretches her hand only to her Father's friends. Not Shelley, not Wordsworth himself, ever drew so close to the heart of Nature as did the Seraph of Assisi, who was close to the heart of God.

Yet higher, yet further let us go. Is this daughter of God mortal; can her foot not pass the grave? Is Nature, as men tell us, but a veil concealing the Eternal,

> A fold
> Of Heaven and earth across His Face,

which we must rend to behold that Face? Do our eyes indeed close for ever on the beauty of earth when they open on the beauty of Heaven? I think not so; I would fain beguile even death itself with a sweet fantasy, if it be no more than fantasy: I believe that in Heaven is earth. . . . For beauty—such is my faith—is beauty for eternity.

What for Shelley was more of a longing than a certainty was in Thompson's mind an unshakable belief. Even if the biblical promise of "a new heaven and a new earth" and of the resurrection of the flesh does not soften sorrow at the frailty of earthly things, it does at any rate make clear that this frailty is only provisional. In the end man finds, not annihilation, but perfect being. Death is only a gate leading to eternal beauty. Thus the poet can call death itself beautiful: "It is the falling star that trails light after it. It is the breaking wave, which has power. It is the passing shower that lets the rainbow appear."

The greatest symbol for Thompson is the setting sun, which he addresses in one of his magnificent odes as follows:

> If with exultant tread
>   Thou foot the Eastern sea,
>   Or like a golden bee
> Sting the West to angry red,
> Thou dost image, thou dost follow
>   That King-maker of Creation,

Who, ere Hellas hailed Apollo,
    Gave thee, angel-god, thy station;
Thou art of Him a type memorial.
    Like Him thou hang'st in dreadful pomp of blood
       Upon thy Western rood;

      . . . .

Thus hath He unto death His beauty given:
And so of all which form inheriteth
    The fall doth pass the rise in worth;
For birth hath in itself the germ of death,
    But death hath in itself the germ of birth.
It is the falling acorn buds the tree,
The falling rain that bears the greenery,
    The fern-plants moulder when the ferns arise.
    For there is nothing lives but something dies,
And there is nothing dies but something lives.

The passage has the effect of a poetic commentary on the statements in Scripture that the seed must fall into the earth and die in order to bring forth fruit, and that the death of his saints is beautiful in the eyes of God.

Seen in this light, nature gains a new radiance. The poet reads it as a cryptogram of its Creator, and recognizes the hidden player of the cosmic music by his harmonies. He is convinced that without the joyous phenomena of the creation we men can only divine the value of heaven through sheer negations of this common earth, just as, for the blind, light may perhaps be merely the vague opposite of darkness. For Thompson, created things are a sort of refracting atmosphere through which he sees the sun of heaven before it climbs over the mournful horizon of our finite firmament. Indeed he sees nature as a titanic, primeval liturgy, and likes to evoke it in images drawn from religious ritual. An example is the *Orient Ode*, in which the priest Day, in his pontifical vestments, walks in solemn procession through the sanctuary of the East up to the tabernacle and slowly raises the host—the sun—then lays it in the evening, when Twilight, the violet-robed acolyte, takes off his stole, in the shimmering monstrance of the West. Another example is the *Corymbus for Autumn*, in which he hears the calm hour striking the golden gong of the sun and sounding a summons to even-song "in tones of floating and mellow light"; sees "the cowlèd Night" kneeling "on the Eastern sanctuary-stair"; smells the fragrance of incense streaming from the clouds thrown up by the mighty unknown spirit who, as solemn thurifer, "swingeth the slow earth before the embannered throne".

The sum of Thompson's wisdom and the climax of his religious poetry is *The Hound of Heaven*. What an image: God the hound, man the quarry. Man flees from God down the nights, down the days, down the arches of the years, down the labyrinthine paths of his own spirit. He hides from him in the mist of tears and in hasty laughter. He rushes abruptly down the titanic gloom of bottomless fears, away from the heavy footsteps that never cease to follow him. But they echo in unhurried pursuit, with easy steps, moderate speed and majestic suddenness, and a voice echoes—more sudden than the steps: "All things betray thee, who betrayest Me." But Man is afraid that, having God, he will not be allowed to have anything else. The chase goes on, out over the edge of the world, between moon and stars. And the voice echoes on: "Naught shelters thee, who wilt not shelter Me." He flees to the eyes of little children; their angel plucks them back from him. He flees to the secrets of nature; they give him no comfort. Nature, a poor stepmother, cannot assuage his thirst; never has milk from her contented his thirsty mouth. The hunt comes closer: "Lo! naught contents thee, who content'st not me." Naked, he awaits the blow from the raised hand of God's love. He kneels without any protection. The voice is all round him like a bursting sea:

> Lo, all things fly thee, for thou fliest Me!
>
> . . . .
>
> Whom wilt thou find to love ignoble thee
> Save Me, save only Me?

All which I took from thee I did but take,
    Not for thy harms,
But just that thou might'st seek it in My arms.
    All which thy child's mistake
Fancies as lost, I have stored for thee at home:
    Rise, clasp my hand, and come!

Is my darkness, asks Man vanquished by God's love, in the end the shadow of his hand, stretched out caressingly?

    Ah, fondest, blindest, weakest,
    I am He Whom thou seekest!
Thou dravest love from thee, who dravest Me.

So this is Thompson's wisdom: Nature withdraws from the godless and creation eludes his grasp. But he who loves God finds the longed-for earth in heaven; it is more beautiful than he thought, freed of every stain, as glorious as on the first day. It is Franciscan wisdom: St Francis abandoned all and gained all. He knew that he had to seek the Kingdom of God first, and that then everything else would be added to him. He also knew the truth of that other saying: Everything belongs to you, for you belong to God. His flight from the world became an affirmation of the world. Thompson not only respected St Francis; he followed him in his poverty. His wisdom is the wisdom of suffering. This sets the seal of greatness on his powerful poetry.

PROPHECY

Newman (1801–90)

As a religious thinker Newman stands beside Augustine and Pascal. As a prose-writer he is second to none in the English language: "He drew from the resources of English a greater and richer variety than any writer since Shakespeare's day" (May).

Newman's thought bears a very personal stamp, and his literary work is largely autobiographical. Not only does he express his own thought in his wonderful *Apologia pro Vita Sua*, in the novel *Loss and Gain*, and in diaries, letters and lyric poems (one of which, the hymn *Lead, Kindly Light*, has become the common property of all English-speaking Christian communities); even his sermons and his historical and theological essays are fragments of a great confession. Newman is fond of the dialogue, in which "heart speaks to heart", and he therefore often casts a learned exposition in the form of a letter, addresses his friends and opponents directly in historical and doctrinal discussions, and gives even systematic essays the character of a dialogue. All this helps to influence the reader in favour of Newman, who is a truly existential thinker.

But what makes him great is the fact that this gifted man did not remain in subjectivism, but early on took firm hold of objective reality and never let go of it again throughout his life. Newman was a man of delicate and lively feelings, but he was by no means a romantic or a fanatic. He had no sympathy for exaggerated emotion and always displayed remarkable objectivity. He was fond of the natural sciences, won a prize at Oxford for mathematics, and toyed with the idea of becoming an engineer. He became convinced quite early in his life that religion was not an affair of vague emotions, but was concerned with objective reality, a reality which had a dogmatically definable content.

In adopting this position the young Anglican clergyman came into conflict with the religious liberalism which was beginning to gain ground in England at that time. What Newman fought against in liberalism was the anti-dogmatic principle. He explained when he was a cardinal: "Liberalism in religion is the doctrine that there is no definite, binding religious truth, but that on the contrary one creed is as good as the other. This doctrine is daily gaining ground and strength. It cannot be reconciled with the recognition of *one* religion as the true one. Liberalism teaches that all religions should be tolerated, for every religion is simply a question of point of view. According to this theory, revealed religion is not a truth but an emotional feeling and a matter of taste; it is not an objective fact, a marvel; it is the right of every individual to say whatever his imagination suggests to him. Surrender need not be based unconditionally on faith. One may go to the Protestant and to the Catholic church; one can obtain good from both without belonging to either of them."

Newman saw clearly what lay behind liberal phraseology. "Religion is a private affair. We all believe in the same God. I too believe in a higher being, but I am not bound by the tenets of any particular Church." Such views lead to "simple scepticism".

Newman saw with horror that the liberal spirit was penetrating the Anglican Church. He also noticed that increasing worldliness was weakening the essential Christianity of the clergy. He did not mince his words in a forthright attack on the domesticated Anglican priesthood:

> Here are Servants of Christ with huge incomes, with splendidly furnished houses, with wives and children, solemn stewards and liveried servants. They give parties in the best style, are condescending and gracious, wave their hands and weigh their words as if they were the salt of the earth, and there is nothing to remind us of their calling but their black coat and white tie. . . . Quite obviously the first goal for all of them is to enjoy life. God only comes second. It goes without saying that they all want to go to heaven in the end, but for the time being they want to live comfortably, marry, earn money, secure a position, have a nice house and so on.
>
> Such preachers of the Gospel are no longer worthy of belief.

Newman looked into the future with wide open eyes. His *Prophecy of the Further Development of the World* paints a gloomy picture: "I always thought that a period of widespread unbelief would come, and in fact through the years the waters have risen like a flood. I see the time coming, after my death, when only the tops of the mountains will still be visible, like islands in the waste of waters." And again: "What lies before us? I look upon the coming generation with melancholy sympathy and almost with a shudder." And again: "The next generation and the one after that will experience a dreadful time. The devil is loose." Newman's view of the world was eschatological and apocalyptic. Characteristically he was concerned with a problem quite alien to his own century, with its faith in progress: the problem of the Antichrist. In the midst of the self-satisfied complacency of the Victorian age his prophetic words sounded strange. He was far in advance of his age, and consequently could not be understood by it. Again and again his views were opposed and rejected. He strode through his century in lonely greatness. He shared the lot of so many prophets whose words have only been understood by a later generation. Copeland wrote retrospectively: "It can be seen how Newman warned us in a kind of prophetic preview of the impending tests and struggles, of the confusion and dangers which at that time seemed obscure and unregarded and have since been experienced by our present age. It almost seems as if it was his vocation to warn us of these things and at the same time to have consolation and encouragement ready, to offer a spiritual sheet-anchor for the coming storm."

"Where Newman as a religious thinker looks to the future is in his un-domesticating of a domesticated Christianity, his destruction of a safely middle-class Christianity, a safely Christian middle-class. Only an undomesticated God, an undomesticated Christ can seriously challenge the atheism of the undomesticated masses" (Söhngen).

Newman had no illusions, but he was not timid or cowardly either. He had a deeply rooted faith that was confident of victory, and he was tirelessly active in the consciousness of a God-given mission. His prayer is evidence of this:

O God, the time is full of trouble. The cause of Christ seems almost lost. And yet—never did Christ stride more mightily over the earth, never was his coming clearer, never was his presence more perceptible, never was his service more pleasant. Therefore in these moments of eternity between the storms of earth let us pray to thee: O God, thou canst lighten the darkness, and thou alone.

The following admission is also noteworthy.

In the medieval (period), since Catholicism was then the sole religion recognized in Christendom, unbelief necessarily made its advances under the language and the guise of faith; whereas in the present . . . unbelief throws off the mask . . . and confronts us in the broad light and with a direct assault. And I have no hesitation in saying . . . that I prefer to live in an age when the fight is in the day, not in the twilight; . . . It is one great advantage of an age in which unbelief speaks out, that Faith can speak out too. . . . The sway of the Church is contracted, but she gains in intensity what she loses in extent. . . . Secular advantages no longer present an inducement to hypocrisy. (University Subjects, Sec. V, pp. 381–5.)

With bold realism Newman threw himself into the struggle for the spiritual renewal and strengthening of Christianity. His first means was his *Sermons*, which were unusually successful. Newman has been described as "one of the most powerful preachers that Christianity has produced". An eye-witness says: "The most wonderful thing of all was the complete elimination of his own personality . . . every one of his sermons thus became a sermon on the objectivity of the revealed truth." This is confirmed by another contemporary: "His sermons made the hearer think of what the speaker was saying, and not of the sermon or the preacher." Newman emitted considerable power from the pulpit:

The force of his personality appeared above all in the new and unusual way in which he brought to life old truths which all Christians knew but most no longer felt. When he spoke, how new the old truth became once again! How it plucked at one's heart in a never previously suspected way! How gently and yet how powerfully he laid his finger on a spot in the listener's heart and told him things about himself that he had not known before. He could express the profoundest truths, to explain which philosophers would have used long words and written many pages, as though by the way, in a few sentences of the simplest English. How delicate his style is and yet how strong! How simple, yet how rich in thought!. How homely, yet how noble! (Shairp).

Newman used all the rhetorical devices of which he was such a master in the service of one single aim: the reform of man. He did not demand obedience to this or that command; instead, he worked for the transformation of a man's whole mental attitude. He did not moralize, nor was he a thunderer or tub-thumper. "He had neither the ability nor the desire to startle or confound his hearers; but he was a master of the art of gently but profoundly disturbing their complacency" (Bremond). "To be complacent means to be in danger."

Newman extended the effect of his sermons, which were printed at the time, through his *Tracts for the Times*. In these he recalled in powerful language truths of faith which had been forgotten, and lashed those who had betrayed religion to the spirit of the times. These *Tracts* made Newman the spiritual leader of the Oxford Movement, which was striving for a renewal of the Anglican Church in the spirit of the primitive Church. Newman was convinced that the true Church had to correspond in its qualities to the primitive Church, that is, it had to be Catholic and apostolic. For Newman saw in the Church of the first four centuries the realization of the Christian ideal. He regarded the early Church as the obligatory norm, from which Rome and Protestantism had departed by distorting the teaching of the apostles with wanton additions. In his work *Via Media* he praised the Anglican Church as the true mean between the extremes of Roman Catholicism and Protestantism. The Anglican Church alone, he said, was based on the primitive Church. The theory of the *Via Media* was shaken by some unpleasant experiences and above all by Newman's thorough historical investigations into the first centuries of the Christian Church (*The Church of the Fathers*; *The Arians of the Fourth Century*; *Translation of Athanasius, with Commentary*). It finally collapsed like a house of cards under the weight of the facts. Gradually Newman became convinced that the Anglicans were schismatics and heretics like the false leaders of antiquity, and that the true Church was that of Rome.

His last doubts departed while he was working on his book *On the Development of Christian Doctrine*. "No doctrine is defined until it is violated." Only heresies made it necessary to formulate the doctrine of the Trinity. Similarly "the concept of the blessed Virgin was developed by the Roman Church with the progress of time. This also happened with all the other Christian concepts." The human spirit can only gradually grasp revelation in the course of time. "New dogmas" are in the last analysis only "truths that have become conscious." It is a question, not of additions and distortions, but of a development which does not obscure earlier knowledge but illuminates it; does not corrupt it, but strengthens it. Revelation unfolds step by step throughout history. Future developments were implicit at the start, and the old is preserved in what comes later. There is therefore no pure Church at the beginning and no distorted Church of later times. The Church of the Fathers is not an exclusive terminus, but the beginning of revelation; not an unsurpassable norm, but a first stage. The question now arises, what distinguishes true development from deformity, excrescence and decay? The most important guarantee of true development, and also of the cohesion of the Church in all ages and in every land, and thus of its apostolic and Catholic character, its unity, is the infallible authority of the Chair of Peter. "Either an objective revelation has not been granted, or it has been provided with the means to impress its objectivity on the world." Earlier, Newman had despised Rome as the religion of superstition, of antichrist, full of deceit, sophistry, force and immorality. Now he called up a host of witnesses from the first three centuries to show that these modern reproaches had already been cast at the primitive Church. The relationship of the Church to false leaders and the judgement of its opponents on it are the same today as then. This, too, shows that the Roman Church of today is identical with the Church of the Fathers. It always remained the same, while heresies continually altered and split up. The Church of the *Via Media* is only "a paper religion", but the Church of

Rome is the living Church of Christ. *On the Development of Christian Doctrine* was almost completed when Newman drew the practical consequences and, at the age of forty-four, went over to the Catholic Church. "To be deep into history is to cease to be a Protestant."

Newman later described his spiritual path to conversion in a brilliant book: the *Apologia pro vita sua* or *History of My Religious Opinions*. The stimulus that produced this self-portrait was a public attack by the Protestant writer Charles Kingsley on Newman's truthfulness. Never has a man described his life and spiritual development in a more convincing or gripping fashion. Never has the flashing blade of satire been wielded with greater skill. The book bears the stamp of a superior mind and at the same time of an honest and straightforward character. It is one of the great masterpieces of English prose, the only one of Newman's books that brought its author immediate success and the admiration of the whole nation, Catholics and non-Catholics alike. Above all it is the moving testimony of a saintly Christian, comparable only with the *Confessions* of St Augustine.

"With his entry into the Catholic Church Newman did not change his convictions but he did change his front" (O. Karrer). Now he was no longer the opponent of liberalism in religion, but of a nervous, reserved attitude to culture, of Ghetto-Catholicism. With new heart he began to pave the way for the pressingly necessary reunion of the Church and Culture, of theology with the other branches of knowledge. The long-standing division had done neither side any good. Culture had been widely affected by materialism, and Catholicism was saddled with the reproach of backwardness. "I have not the slightest doubt that the Catholic Church and its teaching originate from God; but I also recognize clearly that in certain circles a spiritual narrowness prevails that does not come from God," wrote Newman at the time.

His practical efforts in Dublin and Oxford to raise the intellectual level of English Catholicism remained outwardly unsuccessful, but his thoughts were preserved in literary form so that they could be fruitful for a later generation.

First and foremost come the lectures which Newman delivered in Dublin as rector of the Catholic University and which appeared as a book under the title *The Idea of a University*. Newman saw clearly that the attempt to preserve the faith of students by fencing them off from the world only produces the opposite result. A university "is not a Convent, it is not a Seminary; it is a place to fit men of the world for the world. We cannot possibly keep them from plunging into the world . . . but we can prepare them against what is inevitable; and it is not the way to learn to swim in troubled waters, never to have gone into them." Newman regarded a limited and narrow mental attitude and ignorance of the ways of the world not as unavoidable concomitants of spiritual illumination but as dangers to faith. For this reason he championed a liberal education that included the study of secular literature. For him, there was no conflict between religion and knowledge.

Newman also played an important part as a contributor, and for a time editor, in the publication of the *Rambler*, a literary periodical for the Catholic laity. Supporting intellectual freedom and social and political progress, it aimed at leading English Catholicism out of the ghetto. It was for the *Rambler* that he wrote his essay *On Consulting the Faithful in Matters of Doctrine*. Violently attacked at the time, today it has been abundantly justified—another indication that Newman was far in advance of his age. With his genuinely priestly temperament, Newman had no time for the clerical contempt for the laity which was the fashion in his day. He opposed all clergymen who aimed at "keeping laymen at arm's length". Of set purpose he championed the lay element in the Church. He took the view that laymen should not simply follow the injunctions of the clergy like dumb animals; they too were members of the Church and called to apostolic co-operation.

Newman's greatest achievement was his justification of Christianity in the face of modern unbelief. The desire to prove that the Christian faith gives man absolute certainty produced his original and pioneering work *An Essay in aid of a Grammar of Assent*. Newman here shows that the act of faith is the result neither of an intellectual process nor of an upsurge of emotion, but of a personal decision by the whole man springing from conscience. Newman's arguments about the function of conscience form the climax of his philosophy of religion. Conscience is "our great inward teacher in the sphere of religion". As the voice of God it speaks not only to our will but also to our cognitive faculty. For Newman conscience is "the basic principle of our intellectual make-up and the supreme binding force of religion" (Laros). Even in the *Open Letter to the Duke of Norfolk,* which defends the infallible authority of the Pope, Newman ends by emphasizing the primacy of conscience: "Certainly if I had to remember religion in drinking a toast—which would hardly be fitting—I should empty my glass, with your permission, to the well-being of the Pope—but first to conscience, and only after that to the Pope." In his struggle with the unchristian spirit of the age, Newman was much assisted by his ability to think himself completely into the intellectual and spiritual situation of his opponents. He could expound alien views so objectively and clearly that Huxley asserted that he could put together a primer of unbelief out of Newman's religious writings. A celebrated example of Newman's objectivity is the passage on the ideal of the gentleman which is often quoted out of context and included in anthologies. The reader who does not know the context thinks that Newman is expounding his own ideal, while in reality he is passing a subtle judgement on a purely worldly education which lacks religion.

Newman's unadorned lives of Antony, Theodore, Chrysostom, Benedict, Augustine and Philip Neri are distinguished by an attractive love of truth. These portraits differ markedly from the sentimental, edifying hagiography of the period with its moralist approach. Since Newman, genuine hagiography can provoke admiration, respect and love, but it can no longer descend to embellishing and touching-up its subject. "David was a man after God's heart, but his great reputation does not oblige us to excuse his adultery or his betrayal of his friend; similarly, we can observe that St Cyril was a great servant of God without feeling compelled to defend certain aspects of his ecclesiastical career. It is not proper to call grey white." Elsewhere in his *Historical Sketches* Newman says of the saints: "The imperfections which they still retain certainly make us love them more without causing us to respect them any the less, and they are a source of comfort in the discouragement and faint-heartedness which can descend on him who, amid error and sin, strives to imitate them."

Newman admitted with the same disarming honesty the innumerable difficulties which the intellectual effort to wrestle with religious questions is bound to bring with it. He wrote to a doubter:

> You must begin every reflection on religion by realizing clearly that from its very nature the question possesses an ineradicable difficulty. . . . No one can accept a theory that does not involve this difficulty. It is bound to occur in one form or the other. If we say, "All right then, I shall believe nothing at all", even this believing in nothing involves a difficulty, an intellectual difficulty. Doubt has its difficulty; the conclusion that there is no such thing as truth has its difficulty; to say that truth exists, but no one can find it; to assert that all religious views are true, or one is as good as the other, also has its difficulty; to say that there is no God; or that there is a God, but he has not revealed himself except in nature, again has its difficulty; and no doubt Christianity involves a difficulty.

Newman is also an exemplary controversialist. Although he had no taste for inter-denominational disputes, the famous convert could hardly escape expressing his opinion on the variations in belief between the different Churches. Yet his Lectures *On Certain Difficulties Felt by Anglicans in submitting to the Catholic Church* and his other relevant writings contain no trace of the renegade's hatred. Long after his conversion Newman wrote:

> I am not speaking of the Anglican Church in any disdain. . . .
> I recognize in the Anglican Church a time-honoured institution,
> of noble historical memories, a monument of ancient wisdom
> . . . a source of vast popular advantage, and, to a certain point,
> a witness and teacher of religious truth. I do not think that, if
> what I have written about it since I have been a Catholic, be
> equitably considered as a whole, I shall be found to have taken
> any other view than this. . . . And as I have received so much
> good from the Anglican Establishment itself can I have the
> heart, or rather the want of charity, considering that it does for
> so many others what it has done for me, to wish to see it over-
> thrown? I have no such wish while it is what it is, and while
> we are so small a body. Not for its own sake, but for the sake of
> the many congregations to which it ministers I will do nothing
> against it. . . . Doubtless the National Church has hitherto been
> a serviceable breakwater against doctrinal errors more funda-
> mental than its own. How long this will last in the years now
> before us, it is impossible to say . . . my own idea of a Catholic's
> fitting attitude towards the National Church in this its supreme
> hour, is that of assisting and sustaining it, if it be in our power,
> in the interest of dogmatic truth. (Appendix to the *Apologia*,
> Everyman ed., p. 267.)

Newman knew, like Augustine, "that there is no false teaching without an admixture of truth". Therefore converts come "not to lose what they have, but to gain what they have not". Newman longed fervently for reunion in the faith. To a non-Catholic Christian he wrote:

> What a mystery it is in our day that there is so much that
> could bring religious people together, and so much that separates
> them from each other! . . . Nothing could be more senseless and
> also less truthful than compromise and artificial Mergers. . . .
> Sad as it is to see on all sides the fruitless longing for Unity of
> which you speak, it is also hopeful. We may hope that our good
> spirit has not inspired pious people with the wish and prayer
> for unity without intending to hear their prayer in his own

time. . . . In the most important points on which you write I can be at one with you. And I rejoice at that as a compensation for the frightful collapse of faith which we see around us. Just as the setting of the sun brings out the stars, so one can see great leading ideas flash out which, while unbelief is winning the day, are greeted by men of different religions as their common property.

The Apologia pro Vita Sua ends with a prayer for the reunification of divided Christendom.

One of Newman's most characteristic works is *The Dream of Gerontius*, a handbook on dying like a Christian in the face of eternity. It is "the poem of a man for whom the vision of the Christian revelation was always very real, influencing action more strongly and busying the imagination more powerfully than all worldly interests put together" (Hutton). This vivid consciousness of the reality of God and heaven was the foundation of Newman's teaching and life. Even in his Anglican period he said in a sermon:

There are two worlds "the visible and the invisible", as the Creed speaks,—the world we see, and the world we do not see. And the world which we do not see as really exists as the world we do see. . . . And yet in spite of this universal world which we see, there is another world . . . quite as close to us, and more wonderful; . . . All round us are numberless objects, coming and going, watching, working or waiting, which we see not: this is that other world which the eyes reach not unto, but faith only. . . . Almighty God exists more really and absolutely than any of those fellow-men whose existence is conveyed to us through the senses. . . . And in that other world are the souls also of the dead . . . angels also are inhabitants of the world invisible, . . . "ministering spirits, sent forth to minister, for them who shall be heirs of salvation" (Heb. 1.14). . . . Persons commonly speak as if the other world did not exist now, but would after death. No, it exists now, though we see it not; it is among us and around us. . . . We hold communion with it and take part in it. . . . We know that to remove the world which is seen, will be the manifestation of the world which is not seen.

We know that what we see is as a screen hiding from us God and Christ, and His Saints and Angels. And we earnestly desire and pray for the dissolution of all that we see, from our longing after that which we do not see. (*Parochial Sermons*, IV, pp. 200 following.)

In another place Newman wrote: "All visible things—world, Bible, Church, civil order and man himself—are symbols and representations and tools of an invisible world, truer and loftier than this visible world." A few years before his death Newman chose as his epitaph: "From shadows and pictures to truth."

Kierkegaard (1813–55)

Between Newman and Kierkegaard, the greatest northern thinkers of the nineteenth century, there are so many resemblances, but also such characteristic differences, that the two have often been compared. Both the Englishman and the Dane were men who, in a painful struggle, realized the truth and reality of Christianity existentially and, as must always happen, especially in the nineteenth century, in opposition to their age and surroundings.

Kierkegaard once imagined the following scene: on the last day God asked a professor if he had sought the Kingdom of God first. The professor answered, no, but he could repeat this verse of the Bible in nine languages. Whereupon he received such a slap on the face from an angel, with the words "You bungler!", that he fled several thousand miles. Elsewhere Kierkegaard expresses the same thought in the lapidary sentence: "It is the misfortune of Christendom to have turned Christianity into a mere doctrine." Kierkegaard calls this development a misfortune because it implies a fateful failure to recognize the true nature of Christianity. "Christianity is not a doctrine but information about life." This exaggerated definition at least contains the truth that Christianity cannot be spread by teaching alone and that it is primarily something else than a doctrine. If Kierkegaard laid the main emphasis on the practical application of Christianity, this approach was particularly justifiable in his century. There were innumerable cases of men talking and writing cleverly about Christianity without believing at all in its truth or living in accordance with their faith. There were many who used daily the vocabulary of Christianity and yet in their hearts were not Christians. Kierkegaard on the other hand demanded existential truth, that is, "above all an active ethical attitude, the expression, exercise and practical realization of what we believe, teach and say" (Haecker).

Thus Kierkegaard can say: "Subjectivity is truth", and "Truth lies in subjectivity." His religious thinking has in fact a strong subjective tinge. Newman on the other hand, whose attitude was likewise by nature individualistic and who himself laid strong emphasis on the decision of the conscience and the personal realization of religion, possessed a strong counterbalance in his conception of the Church, which saved him from the inspired one-sidedness of Kierkegaard. In spite of this we must not be led by the subjective-sounding utterances of Kierkegaard to overlook the fact that he, too, was rooted in the objective facts of salvation. His work is full of brilliant intuitions of great truths; of the truth, for example, that in relation to God man is female and—be he man or woman—"pregnant". Kierkegaard gives us more than the disconnected outpourings of an inwardly elated heart; he grasps firmly what approaches him from outside, from the quite other, and what he has listened for and heard from this source. It is characteristic "that he hears his sentences before he writes them down" (Rest), that he feels as though someone were dictating to him. Kirkegaard conceives himself as a tool that obeys the command: hear and write! This alone gives him an affinity with the prophets. The result is a language of tense beauty and illuminating richness, although it borrows its concepts from a false philosophy, and a work "full of intuitions which are brilliant and true, but devoid of any harmony among themselves" (Haecker).

The great Danish writer was no system-builder, partly from

lack of systematic power, partly from the conviction that truth, and above all religious truth, cannot be caught by a philosophical system. For this reason he turned sharply on Hegel, whose philosophy he regarded as Christianity's worst enemy. Although Kierkegaard's polemic against Hegel itself grew from the soil of the Hegelian philosophy, it drew its strength from other sources. And although Kierkegaard continued to breathe the atmosphere and use the language of the upside-down philosophy of German idealism, by temperament he was diametrically opposed to it. The existentialist philosophy made Kierkegaard's protest ineffective by incorporating it in a system and depriving his work of its Christian premises.

That was Kierkegaard's real mission: in an intellectual world whose stars were Goethe and Hegel, to point to the sun of the living God-man. He had to defend the supernatural against the natural, the transcendence of God against the immanence of rationalism, the personality of God against pantheism, the reality of sin and redemption against enlightened philanthropy and the new humanism. Kierkegaard carried out this mission with immense earnestness. Inexorably he confronted his contemporaries with his *Either-Or*: "One must either resolutely deny, combat and persecute Christianity, or one must really live it. What lies between is the cult of genius and deceit."

This fervent Christian did not possess his faith as a self-evident heritage. It is true that he had been given a strict religious upbringing by his father, but in his formative years he drew away from this austere religion of the cross. It was only after alternating struggles, at one moment against his abysmal melancholy, the next against his despairing pursuit of pleasure, that he attained the unassailable position of the believing Christian. This passionate striving found expression in a number of works, above all in his book *The Concept of Anxiety*, in which Kierkegaard discusses the psychological possibilities of the fall, and in the anonymous writings *Either-Or*, *Fear and Trembling*, *Recapitulation*, and *Stages on Life's Road*, in which he depicts in existential personalities the aesthetic, ethical and religious modes of life. The existence of God is for him beyond doubt; but he is doubtful whether God is good. His inner struggle for salvation is reflected in the six autobiographical inserts in the *Stages*: *A Possibility*, *Quiet Despair*, *The Leper*, *Solomon's Dream*, *Nebuchadnezzar*, *Periander*. It is a struggle with the realities of light and darkness.

After his break-through, Kierkegaard began to carry out his "extraordinary mission." He saw his most important task in "so making the springs work, that the old, nothing but the old, shall become new again". He was not interested in giving doctrine a fresh content but in finding a new way of drawing people's attention. He did not wish to confirm the truth of revelation, but to place the reader before a decision, to challenge him to an independent act of acceptance. His whole literary activity revolves round "the problem of how one becomes a Christian."

Especially important are the *Talks*, which are intended as a methodical introduction to the religious and Christian life. The most important series is entitled *Works of Love*.

The aim of these writings is to awaken the reader to the spiritual life and to unmask the pious self-deceit of domesticated Sunday-Christianity. They attack the superficiality and impotence of a comfortable Christianity of habit which has become no more than a string of empty phrases. In face of the relativism of the historical approach prevailing at the time Kierkegaard demands that we become contemporaries of Christ. If we decline to do this, then we are separated from Christ by nineteen hundred years of history or by the distance between earth and heaven. For Kierkegaard, to be a contemporary of Christ means to suffer with Christ. Especially *Sickness unto Death* and *Training in Christianity* portray practical Christianity as the religion of scandal, paradox and the suffering imitation of Christ. They aim at inculcating the heroic attitude, which is admittedly not a possibility for the great mass of men, but only for the individual. Consequently, Kierkegaard's appeal is addressed to the individual.

Kierkegaard wrote in his diary:

Matthew 10.17: "Do not put your trust in men." Man is by nature a brutish creature. All human striving therefore aims at gathering in crowds ("let us unite", etc). Naturally all kinds of fine reasons are adduced: love, sympathy, enthusiasm to accomplish something great, and so on. Such are the usual titles of human, thievish hypocrisy. The truth is that in a crowd one is free from the criterion of personality and ideal. The Christian law says on the contrary: either go out into the wilderness, away from men, so that you can keep the criterion, the ideal free from the falsity of number (the quantitative) and the cheating it involves (for counting here means cheating)—or you remain among men; in that case, however, you must suffer persecution in order to preserve the heterogeneousness which protects the personality and the ideal. But direct continuity with the mass is impossible for Christianity.

The individual must be ready to give himself as a sacrifice. This was how Kierkegaard understood his own existence: "Christianity is simply not present in this country; if there is to be even talk of getting it back, a poet's heart must first break, and I am that poet." This did not exclude a passionate attack on the Danish State Church; it is only against this background that Kierkegaard's struggle against Bishop Mynster assumes its real meaning. The conflict with the established Church was as unavoidable for Kierkegaard as it was for Newman. It was a repetition of Christ's collision with the Scribes and Pharisees. That conflict ended with a sacrifice, too.

Furiously Kierkegaard turned against the officials and managers of official Christianity. Professors, clergy and church officials had made Christianity the subject of learned dispute, historical contemplation, objective admiration, private enthusiasm or earthly business.

Kierkegaard was provoked by this into challenging these so-called Christians in a series of violently polemical articles. In general tenor, one-sided simplification of the issues and brilliance of language, *The Moment* can be compared with

Pascal's *Provincial Letters*. "This is the position of Christianity: the State paternally appoints a thousand officials by examination, and Christianity is submerged in talk." Kierkegaard felt irresistibly impelled to sound the alarm: "Christendom has done away with Christianity without really noticing what was happening; consequently, if we want to accomplish anything, we must try to re-introduce Christianity into Christendom."

In his moral fury, his holy wrath, Kierkegaard became the inexorable judge of his age and of Christendom, resembling in many respects the ancient prophets. But he forgot that the Church is like a net that catches all kinds of fish, or like a field in which weeds grow beside the wheat; that in spite of the rotten fish and the weeds it is a holy net and a holy field; and that only at the end of the world will the wicked be separated from the just.

All the same, Kierkegaard's literary work acted as a necessary corrective to the degenerate thought and action of his contemporaries. The idea of a corrective plays an important part in which weeds grow beside the wheat; that in spite of the Protestantism; nevertheless he allowed himself to criticize Luther and Protestantism. For we must not turn the corrective into the norm, or everything will be thrown into confusion. "Are not Protestantism and Luther's achievements really a corrective? And has not great confusion arisen because they have been made into a set of regulations?" We can apply the idea of the corrective to Kierkegaard's own work and thus gain a clearer idea of its meaning and limitations.

His spiritual dialectic made Kierkegaard the ancestor of many different currents of thought and schools in the twentieth century: depth psychology, dialectical theology, and the existential philosophy of Jaspers, Heidegger, Sartre and Marcel. He inspired Protestant thinkers like Barth and Tillich, and Catholic thinkers like Guardini, Przywara, Haecker and Dempf. He may often be unjustifiably invoked, and the renewed interest in him may be based on some fundamental misunderstandings, but it remains true that Kierkegaard's corrective still retains considerable power even today.

Dostoevsky (*1821–81*)

Since the First World War Dostoevsky, like Kierkegaard, has won world-wide respect as a prophetic thinker who was far in advance of his age and already struggling with the questions that shake the twentieth century. It is not only Russian philosophers like Nikolai Berdyaev, Leo Shestov, Vyacheslav Ivanov, A. L. Wolynski, Vassili, Rozanov, Fedor Stefun and Dimitri Merezkovsky who have been decisively influenced by him. In England Arnold Bennett learnt from him; and in France André Gide. There is not one important German writer, philosopher or theologian of the last fifty years who did not receive something essential from him. Thomas Mann, Hermann Hesse, Ernst Jünger, Werner Bergengruen, Romano Guardini, Erich Przywara, Theodor Steinbüchel, Alois Dempf, Paul Simon, Theoderich Kampmann, Edward Thurneysen, Sigmund Freud, Möller van den Bruck—different as they are, they all felt attracted by the exciting world of Dostoevsky.

For it is a whole world that unfolds before the reader's eye in the great novels *Crime and Punishment, The Idiot, The Possessed, Raw Youth* and *The Brothers Karamazov*. At first glance it seems to be a confused, chaotic, twilight world, but closer acquaintance brings recognition of the spiritual order underlying it. In figures like Raskolnikov, Stavrogin, Kirilov, Werchovensky, Smerdyakov and Ivan Karamazov he portrayed nihilism with psychological accuracy and metaphysical depth. His personal spiritual experience assisted him. For Dostoevsky himself had traversed the wilderness of nihilism. "My Hosanna has passed through the cleansing fire of doubt," he confessed, and as a young man he wrote in a letter: "I am a child of this age, a child of unbelief and doubt." As a radical and atheistic socialist, in the novel *Poor People* he wrote the chief work of the early socialist literature of Russia. For taking part in a political conspiracy he was exiled to Siberia. The suffering of the years in Siberia transformed him. Living among convicts, he came to know the religious powers in the Russian people. "From them I took back into my soul the Christ whom I had learnt to know in my parents' house and then lost."

The mature Dostoevsky felt himself a son of the Orthodox Church. But that did not prevent him from seeing the defects of the Orthodox Church: "Since the time of Peter the Great our church has been crippled." He also criticized the materialistically-minded popes. Indeed he directed still more serious accusations against Western Christendom, which, he said, had betrayed Christ and distorted him until he was unrecognizable. Europe he saw as one vast cemetery, and while middle-class civilization enjoyed its belief in progress he could already sense the distant flood driving everything to destruction. Dostoevsky's novels and stories, his *Letters* and his *Journal of an Author* are full of gloomy prophecies: "Never was Europe so full of hostile elements as in our time; it is as though there were dynamite under everything, waiting only for the spark to touch it off." Dostoevsky saw "calamity impending over the whole of Europe", and considered that the outbreak of a world war could not be far away. Russia, too, he said, had reached a terminus, and was hanging over an abyss. An apocalyptic feeling filled the seer: "The world will only be saved after it has been visited by the evil spirit. The evil spirit is near. Our children will perhaps see it."

In his politico-metaphysical novel *The Possessed* Dostoevsky described and unmasked Bolshevism fifty years before the beginning of the Russian revolution. His inspired picture of revolutionary and totalitarian methods anticipates with horrifying accuracy the happenings of our time. It has rightly been pointed out that the Russian revolution followed the precise course predicted by Dostoevsky. So clear is the parallel between the novel and the historical events that the writer has been celebrated in Russia as a prophet and harbinger of the Bolshevist system.

A discontented intellectual founds a communist cell. Reciprocal spying, denunciation and common crimes weld the members, when they try to break away, into a community bound by oath. The "possessed" deliberately undermine society by means of pamphlets, oral propaganda, scandals, strikes, riots, terror and assassinations until it is ripe for complete overthrow. The destruction of moral standards and the family can only further this process: "Our supporters are not only the fire-raisers and murderers. The teacher, too, who laughs with the children at their God and their home-life, is one of us. The lawyer who defends the educated murderer with the argument that the murderer was more cultivated than his victim is one of us." After the "seizure of power" the masses are to be handled in accordance with the following programme: "Complete obedience, deprivation of will-power, reduction to the condition of a flock of sheep by means of a new education, re-education of whole generations." All these measures "are based on scientific facts". Their consequences are these: "First of all, the level of education falls. We need no higher talents! They are either banished or executed. We need no education; obedience must spread first. The thirst for education is itself an aristocratic impulse. Everything is reduced to a common denominator." Opponents are liquidated. Shatov, who has become restless, is shot by his comrades one foggy night, Kirilov is driven to suicide by Werchovensky and there is nothing left for Stavrogin but a well-soaped silk cord.

Dostoevsky does not restrict himself to painting a vivid picture of the revolution; he also shows how this state of affairs arises. His real achievement consisted in laying bare the spiritual roots of Bolshevism and in thus showing it up for what it was, a satanic temptation of mankind, which longs for salvation. The harm begins with the unrealistic desire for an earthly paradise of the sort dreamed of by Werchovensky in *Raw Youth*, Stavrogin in *The Possessed* and Ivan Karamazov in the *Legend of the Grand Inquisitor*. Socialism believes that it can make the dream of Utopia a reality through science and technology. Human reason is powerful enough, it maintains, to master nature and to guide history in accordance with its own plans. Reason takes the place of the divine providence and government of the world. The engineer Kirilov is a symbol of modern technology which aims not only at worldly but at cosmic domination, and boasts of dethroning God with artificial moons and planets and making Christ superfluous by means of penicillin and an increased old age pension: "He who conquers pain and fear will himself become God. Then there will be a new life, a new man, everything will be new. . . . The history of the world will be divided into two periods: from gorilla to the annihilation of God, and from the annihilation of God to—"—"To gorilla?"—"to the physical transformation of the earth and man. Man will be God and will alter physically. The whole Universe will be altered, everything will alter, all thoughts and emotions." Rationalism, utilitarianism, materialism, and, above all, atheism form the basis of the revolution: "Socialism is not just a question for the workers, for the fourth estate; it is above all a question of atheism, a question of making atheism effective in the present, of the tower of Babel, which is erected without God, not in order to reach from earth to heaven, but to bring heaven down to earth." This titanic project is a product of eighteenth-century rationalism and of liberalism. Dostoevsky's revolutionaries simply carry to their logical end in nihilism the ideas of their liberal fathers, which had stopped half-way, and draw the practical conclusions—to the horror of the fathers. For in the process the ideals of "liberty, equality and fraternity" turn into the exact opposite. Shigalev sums up his programme in the sentence "I start out from unlimited freedom and end up with unlimited despotism." This doctrine demands equality and in fact produces the dictatorship of some over all. It preaches fraternity and practises hatred and murder. It promises the harmony of an earthly paradise and unleashes the struggle of all against all.

Dostoevsky puts his own attitude to socialism in the mouth of Zosima in *The Brothers Karamazov*: "They will end by drowning the earth in streams of blood. . . . They have proclaimed freedom, but what do we see in their freedom? Nothing but slavery and suicide. They say: 'If you have wants, satisfy them, for you have the same rights as the rich and well-born. Do not be afraid to satisfy them; multiply and intensify them!' That is what they now call freedom. And what is the result of this right to increase wants? Among the rich, isolation, and intellectual and spiritual suicide. Among the poor, on the other hand, hatred and murder, for they were given claims all right, but they were not given the means to satisfy their wants. We are assured that the world will grow ever more united and develop into a brotherly community. . . . Do not believe in this unity of mankind! When freedom is conceived as freedom from restraint and the swift satisfaction of all desires, nature is corrupted." Dostoevsky rejects decisively all attempts to organize life by means of reason alone without God, and to bring about a paradise on earth. For these attempts disregard the reality of God and the essential nature of man. They come to grief on three facts: man's unpredictable freedom, which cannot be suppressed, the inevitability of suffering, and God, the real lord of history. Dostoevsky showed that atheists, precisely because they do not believe in God, have a false conception of man and society, and, if they act logically, are bound to destroy themselves, the family, the people and mankind. There can only be a society worthy of man if God has a place in it. The communist state, with its hostility towards God, is also the enemy of man.

Gloomily as Dostoevsky viewed the future, he was not without hope. The devils had to be driven out of Russia's ailing body, then "the patient will recover and sit at the feet of Jesus." Dostoevsky made his own contribution to the conquest of nihilism by not merely depicting it but also contrasting with the figures of the possessed those of holy men. The proud are overcome by the humble, the pleasure-seeking by the pure, the avaricious by those who have deliberately chosen to be poor. Dostoevsky's work does not only portray crime, vice, perversion and debauchery; it also contains a great deal of goodness and spirituality, and examples of religious, even saintly, life such as the cheerful Zosima, whose wisdom sets many on the right road again; the mystical pilgrim Makar, whose existence is rooted in Mother earth yet points up to heaven; the poor maiden Sonia, whose love overcomes the nihilism of Raskolnikov; Prince Mishkin, who is an idiot, an absolute fool, a fool in Christ, a Russian Don Quixote; and the lovable monastery schoolboy Alyosha, who is called a "cherub". On his own admission Dostoevsky only wrote *The Brothers Karamazov* "to compel people to recognize that a pure, ideal Christian is not just an abstraction but a real and tangible possibility, and that Christianity is the only refuge for Russia from all its woes."

For Dostoevsky, Christianity is not a religion for the individual, but essentially an affair of the community. For this reason he regards the pride of the individualist as the worst sin of all, which can only be atoned for by the humble and public confession of guilt before all men. Dostoevsky was keenly aware that every sin—however "private", secret and confined to thought alone—must have consequences not only for the sinner himself, but also for his fellow men, indeed for the whole world. "All are guilty before all and for all." Men's solidarity in guilt demands solidarity in suffering as well. All must "take the suffering on themselves and by doing so find redemption." Even the suffering of innocent children, the senselessness of which causes Ivan Karamazov to doubt God's goodness and justice, and drives him to rebel against God, gains a meaning: it belongs to the imitation of Christ, who also suffered innocently in order to atone as a proxy for the sins of mankind.

The positive value attributed to suffering by Dostoevsky takes such forms that it has been interpreted as pathological, as a historical phenomenon, or as characteristic of the "Russian soul". But these interpretations overlook the immensely strong affirmation of life which permeates the novelist's work. Dostoevsky loves the earth, praises its holy soil in dithyrambic terms, and betrays again and again a love of the creation that could hardly be warmer. He makes his pilgrim, Makar, say: "Love God's young creation, love it as a whole and every grain of sand in it. Love every leaf, every ray of God. Love animals, love every plant and every thing. If you love every thing, the mystery of God will be revealed to you in things. One day it will be revealed to you, and then you will recognize it more and more every day. And finally you will love the whole universe with a comprehensive, all-embracing love." Dosto-evsky draws the cosmos into solidarity with mankind, as St Paul did before him in his epistle to the Romans, and em-braces all creatures in brotherly love, as St Francis did in his hymn to the sun.

Dostoevsky expressed this attitude, this awareness, admir-ably at the climax of this greatest novel. Alyosha Karamazov hurries out of the monastery into the world outside:

> His jubilant spirit thirsted for freedom, for space and breadth. Above him was the mighty dome of heaven, dotted with silent, sparkling stars. From the zenith to the horizon extended the misty line of the milky way, still only a vague shimmer. . . . It was as though the earthly peace united with the peace of heaven and the mystery of earth brushed that of the stars. Alyosha stood and looked up—and suddenly he cast himself to the ground, as though smitten by a powerful blow, and kissed it, with tears in his eyes. He sobbed, slaked the earth with his tears, and swore furiously, as though beside himself, to love it for ever! "Slake this earth with your tears of joy. . . ." He felt as if invisible threads from all these innumerable worlds of God met together in him, and his whole soul throbbed from the contact with other worlds. He wanted to forgive everyone everything and to ask for pardon, not for himself, but for everyone and everything! . . . And at that moment he felt more and more clearly, became more and more aware, that something firm and unshakable, like the dome of heaven, was entering his soul, taking possession of his mind like an idea, for the rest of his life and all eternity . . . when he fell to the earth he was still a weak youth; he arose again as a warrior armed to meet life. . . . After three days he left the monastery, obedient to the words of the dead Zosima, who had ordered him to live in the world.

There is no trace here of flight from the world, Byzantine spirituality or Manicheism, any more than there is in Makar's speech in *Raw Youth*:

> Do not say: "Sin is powerful, godlessness is powerful, filthy matter is powerful; we are isolated individuals without any power; filthy matter will corrupt us and prevent the completion of our good work." Do not be so timid, children. There is only one salvation: make yourself responsible for the sins of mankind. The fact is, my friend—and you will recognize the rightness of this as soon as you sincerely make yourself responsible for all and everything—that you really are responsible to everyone for everything. But if, in your laziness and weakness, you blame others, you will finally fall a victim to satanic pride and murmur against God. . . . The sight of men's sins raises the question: "Are we to use force or humility and love?" Always decide in favour of humility and love. . . . Loving humility is a mighty force, the most powerful of all; there is nothing comparable to it. Brothers, do not be repelled by men's sins; love men even in sin, for that is a replica of divine love and the summit of earthly love. Love redeems everything, love saves all.

Many scenes in Dostoevsky's novels allow us to glimpse a Kingdom of God which makes the beauty of eternal peace a reality. As Tyciak puts it, "There is a hint of paradise in these scenes. . . . Dostoevsky's paradise is the supernatural realm of love, mercy and forgiveness." The heralds of this new paradise of Christ are spiritual men, children, the gentle, the compassionate and the peaceful. From them joy and light stream out. In their presence the darkness retreats. The world of hostility to God is shattered by humility and love. The gentle in spirit, who embrace the whole world with love, who suffer patiently without complaining, who kneel before the criminal and respect even in the most abandoned man the image of God and a possible saint—these are they who overcome evil.

Dostoevsky's ideal man does not stand alone. He lives in the community of the Church, which is the mystical body of ~ist, the continuation of the Incarnation, inspired spirituality, but also visible reality. It is not of this world, yet it is *in* this world, called and sent to lead the world to Christ. "Our Lord Jesus Christ only came in order to found the Church here on earth. The kingdom of heaven is part of the natural order . . . it is in heaven, but one can only enter it through the Church, which is founded and erected on earth. . . . The Church is in truth authority here on earth; it is destined to rule, and indubitably can have only one aim: to rule the whole world, as indeed the promise tells us." But the rule of the Church is no tyranny; it is the rule of the spirit, of love and of freedom. The Church shall not rule with the "sword of Caesar", or use earthly instruments of power. In the *Legend of the Grand Inquisitor*, Dostoevsky unjustly accused the Catholic Church of taking away man's freedom and betraying Christ. But his accusation sprang from the genuinely Christian conviction that the teaching and grace of Christ must not and cannot be forced on anyone. God does not want marionettes who can be manipulated as he pleases. "The Saviour did not come down from the cross because he did not wish to convert people forcefully by external miracles; he wanted freedom of belief." It should also not be overlooked that the *Legend of the Grand Inquisitor* is by no means purely polemical in tone. It contains a poetically beautiful and moving portrait of Christ that no reader can forget. Dostoevsky had a spiritual relationship with Christ which was nourished from the reading of the Gospels. He admitted: "I was no longer able to imagine men without him." Christ is indeed the secret centre of his thinking and writing. There is no writer in the whole of Christian literature who has made the spirit of the Sermon on the Mount so much his own as Dostoevsky.

Soloviev (1853–1900)

The model on which the character of Alyosha Karamazov was based and the spiritual progenitor of the *Legend of the Grand Inquisitor* was Dostoevsky's youthful friend Vladimir

Soloviev. This universal genius has been described by Szyl-karski as "the greatest philosopher of whom the Slav peoples can boast." According to Pfleger, he is the "forefather of the modern Russian philosophy of religion", for he formulated with exceptional intellectual force the themes to which Berdyaev, Florenski, Bulgakov and Ilyin turned later on.

Soloviev united to a lively intellect and the capacity for systematic thought delicate aesthetic perceptions. The philosopher of religion and theological historian was at the same time a poet who wrote tender love poems shot through with mystical themes. And in his last masterpiece, the *Three Conversations*, Soloviev's art attains the heights only scaled by the greatest thinker and writer of ancient Greece, the divine Plato. His spiritual forebears are the Neo-Platonists, Origen, Augustine, Leibniz, Kant, Hegel and Schelling. What distinguishes his work is the combination of the strongest faith with great boldness in speculation. Once Soloviev had overcome nihilism in his youth he based his thinking unconditionally on Christianity. Among the themes which accompany all the stages of his development the concept of the Kingdom of God occupies the first place. Soloviev sees the history of mankind as a gigantic cosmic drama: the fall divided the creation from the Creator. But God, eternal love, did not abandon the creation to its misery; he leads it on a long, difficult path to the gates of the kingdom of heaven, until it returns to the bosom of the heavenly father.

In order to bind the world, in all its living and developing variety, as organically as possible to its source, Soloviev adopts a second idea which he found in the sapiential books of the Old Testament, in gnostic literature and in Baader: the idea of sophia, the creative wisdom of God. Soloviev's sophiology is closely bound up with his Christology. Christ, God and Man in one person, unites in himself the fallen creation with its Creator and perfects the work of the eternal wisdom. The restoration of the creature to the bosom of the heavenly father is completed in the Church founded by Christ, which Soloviev never at any point in his career regarded as a national Church but always as an ecumenical Church.

In the first stage of his development Soloviev looked upon his own Greek Orthodox Church as the true ecumenical Church. He considered that the Roman Church had turned away from Christ's truth, and that since the schism the keys of the kingdom belonged to the Eastern Church alone. It alone preserved the undistorted truth, but it would finally unite the whole of mankind in itself. "Holy Russia", "the people of God", was called by providence to lead, through its possession of the truth, all mankind towards the Kingdom of God on earth. This orthodox Russian Messianic conviction found its most forceful expression in Soloviev's *Lectures on the Divine Humanity*. Humanity is enthusiastically promised the "Light from the East." The Slavophils (as the representatives of Russian Orthodox Messianism called themselves) honoured Soloviev as the genius who put their ideas together into an imposing system. Dostoevsky's Messianic ideas were decisively influenced by Soloviev.

But as a seeker after truth Soloviev could not close his eyes to the gap that separated the ideal of "Holy Russia" from the miserable reality. The Russian Church had long been divided. How could it still carry out its mission to mankind? Soloviev investigated the causes of the Russian schism and found that it was essentially a case of the part rising against the whole, the partial against the universal, the local against the ecumenical. The Russian Church would not have had to see millions falling away from it had it not itself first fallen away from the universal Church. Through its division from Rome it lost its unity, and through its dependence on an absolutist state its freedom. "The Russian people purchased the pearl of Christian faith covered in Byzantine dust." How can the Christians of the East maintain that the light of pure faith has always burnt only in their Church, when for centuries this light was in danger of being extinguished in the East? Byzantine piety sought exclusively the salvation of the individual soul and renounced the moral regeneration of society, the salvation of the world. It took the view that it was useless to struggle to conquer the world, and better to leave the world and go into the wilderness. The East forgot that the faith which does not produce deeds is a dead faith. Christ founded the Church as a militant Church, which is to overcome evil in every domain of human life. The Church whose whole activity is limited to prayer and contemplation is no longer a militant Church; it must be regarded as a Church that has simply given up the struggle.

Soloviev insists that Christian truth is not only a theoretical wisdom but also the inner force that informs and moulds all practical life both public and private. Christ is not only priest, but also king. He wants to exercise his authority in every domain of human life. Thus Soloviev expressed ideas later proclaimed by Pius XII when he said: "The Church is the life-force of society."

The study of dogma and Church history which Soloviev undertook in the second stage of his development made him realize that the Russian Church was incapable of carrying out her task of establishing God's kingdom on earth. It also undermined his prejudices against the Western Church. Like Newman, Soloviev was led to Rome by historical studies. He now recognized that the Roman Church was the only Church which could found a true theocracy on earth. The man who had perfected the Russian Messianic ideal in its orthodox form ceased to combat the supposedly anti-Christian ways of Rome and became the defender of Peter's Chair as the only divinely-founded centre of all Christendom. Soloviev did not give up his belief in Russia's Messianic mission, but he no longer saw it in the separation from Western Christianity but in the subordination of his people to that Church which rightfully administers the whole legacy of Christ. Precisely by this subordination "Holy Russia" would fulfil its historical mission by laying the foundations of an edifice which would embrace all mankind and make the true rule of God a reality. Soloviev expounds this Catholic Messianic ideal in *The History and Future of Theocracy* and *Russia and the Universal Church*. In these two books he defends the Catholic Faith and the unity of the Church, and makes himself into an enthusiastic champion of reunion. *Russia and the Universal Church*, which is written in French, has been compared to Möhler's classic, *Symbolism*, and Bossuet's *History of the Differences Between the Protestant Churches*. Soloviev wants to free the faith of the Fathers "from the fetters of local division and national egoism". For this reason he wrote many articles opposing megalomaniac nationalism in Russia. Pan-Slavism he regarded as a distortion of the Messianic ideal.

The third and last stage in Soloviev's spiritual development is in complete contrast to the first two stages: he broke with the Messianic ideal in both its Catholic and its orthodox form. Sadly he gave up the hope that the Kingdom of God could be realized in this world. He also gave up the dream of the Russian people's Messianic mission. Instead, Soloviev was filled with a premonition of approaching catastrophe, which was to herald the end of history. He had moved from the Messianic to the apocalyptic view of history: the Kingdom of God could only become a reality in the next world. The power of evil rages on earth. At the end of time the true believers will form only a small minority. The great mass of men will follow the antichrist. Nevertheless the few Christians will defeat the champions of evil. No longer will all mankind share in the glory of Christ, but only this small loyal band.

This view of history found grandiose expression in Soloviev's masterpiece, the *Three Conversations*. These dialogues on good and evil in history "are unique in force of language, skill in characterization, wit and acuteness of thought" (Setschkareff). They have rightly been described by Szykarski as "the most perfect dialogues produced since Plato." Soloviev affirms the necessity of the struggle against evil and rejects Tolstoy's pacifist doctrine that evil should not be resisted by force. The conclusion of the *Three Conversations* is the *Short Account of the Antichrist.* In it Soloviev delivers a warning against the arrogance of the superman deluded by his command of technology into imagining that he is God. Only the belief in miracles and revelation can save a rationalized and mechanized humanity. The writer draws a sinister yet comforting picture of the future: Mongol invasion of Europe, expulsion of the Asiatics, alliance of the European states in a federation, rise of the antichrist, disloyalty of most of Christendom, reunion of the separated Churches, collapse of the godless world and the return of Christ—such are the details of this gripping vision. The most impressive moment approaches when the old man Starez Johannes, as the representative of the Russian Orthodox Church, and Professor Pauli, as the representative of the Protestants, do homage to the Pope Peter: "It shall be he who finally feeds Christ's sheep . . . now we are one in Christ."

Soloviev managed to recognize the primacy of the pope without leaving the Eastern Church. Putting aside all resentment he clung to the religious idea of the primacy which shone forth from the New Testament and the history of the early Church. He accepted the real primacy of a comprehensive episcopal authority, but explained it as a "primacy of love in the Church conceived as love" on the same grounds as those to be found in Newman: Peter (and in him his successors) was thrice asked about love by Jesus before he was given the primacy. "The primacy is therefore a primacy of love in both intention and practice." Thus Soloviev laid particular emphasis on the mystical side of the Papacy without affecting its primacy of jurisdiction. It is noteworthy "that it was Soloviev, an Oriental, who provided the deepest mystical foundation of the papacy" (Tyciak).

"The conservative tradition of the Eastern Church, the actively formative spiritual power of the Catholic Church of the West, the private judgement and personal piety of the Protestant Church must all, in Soloviev's view, be embraced by the *una sancta catholica* of the future" (Steinbüchel).

Péguy (1873–1914)

Charles Péguy was "a great man and a courageous fighter in the bitter intellectual struggles of the day" (E. R. Curtius), a man of "pure and gaily enthusiastic heart" (Klemperer), full of vitality and confidence. "Everything he wrote led to action, and every action was directed towards one goal" (Claudel). This goal was not so much personal salvation as the redemption of all France, all Christendom, all humanity. Redemption or damnation—that for him was the burning question. He was particularly conscious of the need for solidarity: "We must all be saved together! Reach God together! Appear before him together! We must return to our Father's house together. . . . What would he think of us if we arrived without the others, without the others returning too?"

As a young man Péguy turned away from the Church and became first of all a socialist. But even at that time he was fascinated by the question of salvation, of the redemption of France. He sought to answer it in the two manifestoes on *The Socialist State* and *The Harmonious Community*. He has explained in retrospect what Socialism meant for him:

> By the regeneration of industrial morals, by cleaning up factories, we hoped to accomplish nothing less than the temporal salvation of humanity. This will only provoke laughter in those who will not see that Christianity itself, the religion of eternal salvation, is besmirched with this filth, the filth of bad economic and industrial morals; that Christianity itself cannot be cleansed and freed without an economic, industrial revolution; and that there is no better arranged and equipped place of damnation than the modern factory.

When Péguy struggled passionately for justice in the Dreyfus affair, too, his ultimate concern was with the salvation of France. Even in his socialist period he was attracted by the figure of the saint who is connected with his native city of Orleans and who was to accompany his whole life. He wrote his first *Joan of Arc,* a three-act play which sees the real mission of the saint as the conquest of human misery. Joan is obsessed with worry about the salvation of the world; she would like to save humanity from eternal damnation and offers herself up to eternal torment if the damned can thereby be saved. But her struggle is in vain, the misery remains, and the rebel against God is left in despair. This *Joan* already poses a metaphysical question. Socialism could not provide an answer to it, and so Péguy disappointedly turned his back on the Socialist party. He became a disciple of Bergson, who was delivering the first blows against mechanistic materialism and determinism. But for Péguy the searcher the Bergsonian philosophy, too, was only a passing phase. In 1908 the decisive step was taken. Péguy acknowledged that he had found his faith again and was a Catholic.

Now his really creative period began, the period in which he grew to be "the inspiration of a young Christian élite in France, which had overcome its spiritual crisis, crossed the abyss of despair, and reconquered for itself the eternal realities of Christianity" (Nostitz). In his polemical and critical writings Péguy fought against the modern world, which in its mass approach to life had become sterile, devoid of faith and mechanized, and has made money its king in place of God. "The modern world thinks that it has got rid of God. . . . In reality man has never been so hard pressed by God. . . . In earlier times Man could properly call himself Man, because God was called God. Now that God has been displaced, the old hubris has completed its work; the human spirit has lost its foundation, the magnetic needle wavers erratically."

Péguy's poems, too, are concerned with the present—and still more with the future—although they often take long-past events as their starting-point. The three *Mysteries* are not plays with dramatic events, but dialogues and monologues in free verse; the recurrence of definite themes lends them an effect reminiscent of the beat of the ocean. There is a good deal of allegory in them, too. The *Mystery of the Love of Joan of Arc* is a conversation between the young Jeannette, a girl friend and a nun, who represents the Church, in the Burgundian countryside. It centres round the old theme: why is there so much fruitless suffering? There is an inner struggle in Joan's soul: will she rebel against God, will she despair, or will she become the saint, "who succeeds". The complaint at the lasting misery of damnation persists, but it is no longer rebellion. Joan shares Christ's sufferings and enters the community of saints, which exists to save sinners.

In the sublime *Mystery of Hope* we are introduced to "the little maiden Hope", who is apparently led by her two big sisters, Charity and Faith, but in reality pulls them along with her. Hope leads us to eternal salvation. That is also the message of the *Mystery of the Holy Innocents.*

In the centre of Péguy's thinking and writing stands Christ. The incarnation of the Son of God is for him the event that changed everything and brought into the world "the only order there has ever been in it." It is the theme of *Eva*, Péguy's poetic masterpiece. This verse epic deals in 2000 stanzas, each consisting of four Alexandrines, with the drama of humanity's salvation. It is a series of grandiose pictures. The whole history of the pre-Christian era leads up to the incarnation of Christ. Thanks to the Incarnation Man has been given the possibility of saving the transitory creation for eternity. As a believing Christian Péguy accepts the earth and the resurrection of the flesh. The earthly religiosity of his poetry has the effect of a final defeat of Jansenism. This is particularly apparent in the *Presentation of the Land of Beauce to Our Lady of Chartres*, one of his most beautiful poems, and in the *Tapestry of Saint Genevieve and Joan of Arc*, dedicated to the patron of Paris and the patron of France.

Péguy was killed in the Battle of the Marne, but his spirit lived on. Bernanos said: "I regard Péguy not exactly as a saint, but as a man who, even after his death, remains accessible to every one of us; he always answers when he is needed." Immediately after the war, in 1918, Ernst Robert Curtius made him known in Germany as a "pioneer of the new France". But

Péguy has only really been discovered since 1944, thirty years after his death, when books on Péguy by Romain Rolland, Jean Delaporte and André Rousseaux appeared. In Germany he has been championed by Oswalt von Nostitz, Hans Urs von Balthasar and Karl Thieme. He is regarded today as "the most genuine and talented writer in the European literature" of his time (Romain Rolland).

Bloy (1846–1917)

Like Péguy, Bloy lost his faith when he was a young man. The novel *The Despairer* describes the condition in which he lived at that time: "He was a despairer, but one of those sublime despairers who cast their hearts into heaven." As with Péguy, it was hope that led Bloy back to faith. He confessed in a letter: "I call myself in my book 'the despairer'; that is an ironic title, for there has never been a more incurable hoper than me."

Bloy repeatedly called himself a "pilgrim of the absolute". He regarded it as his task to see and estimate the world only from the point of view of the absolute, to keep confronting men with it, and thereby to force them to a decision. This fervent striver after holiness was so obsessed with the fear that his generation might be lost for ever that he broke out into terrible curses and almost convulsive screams against any person and any institution not concerned as he was with the absolute. His crude strength and merciless honesty worked sometimes like a raging conflagration, at others like a purifying storm. This great radical has been compared to an "island erupting fire in the midst of a sea of icy loneliness" (Fussenegger). We are shocked by the violence of his contempt and cannot help wondering whether it does not contradict Christian love. Bloy himself said, "My most violent pages were written out of love." And again: "If I was a pamphleteer, it was from indignation and love." And on another occasion: "My wrath is the child of a presentiment, extending into the infinite, of things still to come. . . . My wrath is the upsurge of my compassion." When we read Bloy, we are reminded of Christ struggling against the Pharisees, or of Luther's grobianism. His writings are the sorrowful cry of a man who, in an age of unbelief, wants his contemporaries to believe in Christ as the Son of God, who feels his own powerlessness to produce any effect, and who is seized with horror at the thought of the punishments to come.

Even his own contemporaries saw in him the prophetic charisma. "In those days we hardly read the prophets, but we heard an echo of their voices in that of Léon Bloy. . . . Like the prophets, he is impatient to see God's justice revealed on earth" (R. Maritain).

Bloy saw himself as a prophet:

I am one of those who cry in the wilderness and devour the roots of the burning bush when the ravens forget to bring them nourishment. Whether people listen to me or not, whether they are with me or insult me, so long as they do not kill me I shall be the spokesman of revenge and the very obedient servant of a higher wrath that commands me to speak. It is not in my power to give up this service, and I say that with the bitterest sadness. I suffer violently, and the outbreaks of wrath to which I give vent are only the infinitely weakened echo of a higher curse whose mouthpiece I must unfortunately be. No doubt that is why I have had to suffer so much.

In another place Bloy says: "'I came to scatter fire on the earth; I could hardly help wanting it to burn.' Those are the words of Christ in the Gospel. Every Catholic thus has the right and the duty to be a firebrand. . . A society threatened with decay needs fire, and fire alone." On another occasion he confesses: "I am a witness. My task is to give testimony in an age of universal loss of faith." He wrote in his diary in 1900: "I obey a higher command, as the man on the eve of the destruction of Jerusalem did, of whom Josephus speaks. I shall carry on until, like him, I am crushed." And in 1902 he said: "Present events are really horrifying. We are at the prologue of a drama of a sort that will not have been seen for twenty centuries, and I urge you to a certain measure of recollection."

The legend of Bloy's intolerance and fanaticism is refuted by the correspondence with his Calvinist friends in Geneva. His greatest anger was reserved for his own co-religionists, for lukewarm Catholics. "Our self-satisfied Catholics consider themselves pillars of society because they cannot literally be described as scoundrels; but in reality they form the retinue of the princes of this world. It is their mediocrity that attracts the thunderbolt. Today we need apostles, not conference-attenders; witnesses, not word-spinners." In *The Weeping Woman* and *The Life of Mélanie,* Bloy interprets the appearances of the Blessed Virgin at La Salette as the writing on the wall for lukewarm Catholics. The Mother of God weeps because she can no longer restrain the avenging arm of her Son.

On the surface Bloy's work is restless and stormy, but underneath there is the majestic peace of unshakable faith. He attached great value to prayer and gained the insight of a mystic into many mysteries of faith. This is the positive side of his books. Living as he always did in great need, he was particularly filled with the mystery of poverty and suffering.

> Since my childhood I cannot remember ever living without suffering in every way. That is simply a sign that God loves me. . . . I am the anvil in the depths of the abyss, the anvil of God, who lets me suffer because he loves me. . . . Christ healed the eyes of the blind symbolically with dirt and spittle. Therefore let us not pity ourselves too much. If I had not had to lead the existence of a poor wretch, I should not have come to know the hardships of the world. I could not have become their recorder.

In the book *The Poor Man's Blood* Bloy made himself the spokesman of the exploited and the wretched, the accuser of capitalism and colonialism. But he renounces social reforms, because poverty is a mystery.

In *Salvation through the Jews* he attacks anti-Semitism, investigates the fundamental causes of the Jewish destiny and casts light into the abyss of the mystery of the Jewish people.

He is moved simultaneously by boundless contempt and boundless respect for this people—an attitude which corresponds to its paradoxical position. The phenomena of poverty and Judaism were illuminated for Bloy by the idea of community and atonement by proxy.

Bloy emphasized again and again that he was no writer, and it is true that he had little of the artist about him. His hunger for truth was too great for aesthetic questions to bother him. Many objections can be raised to the style and taste of his writings. Nevertheless they were extremely influential. Bloy's formally imperfect novel, *The Woman Who Was Poor*, was informed by a spirit which inspired later Catholic novelists such as Mauriac, Bernanos, Green, Estang, Morel, Waugh, Greene and Böll. Bloy brought home to them what Christ himself had taught: that lost sons and fallen daughters can be nearer to God than the righteous, the well-fed Sunday Christians. Maeterlinck wrote of *The Woman Who Was Poor*: "I regard this work as the only one produced in our day showing clear signs of genius, if by genius we understand certain dazzling flashes of light which link the visible to the invisible and the as yet uncomprehended to what we shall comprehend one day." Raïssa Maritain tells us how, together with Jacques Maritain, she found herself confronting "the reality of Christianity for the first time in that incomparable novel, *The Woman Who Was Poor*." The founder of Neo-Thomism and his wife became Bloy's friends and, after they had been converted to Catholicism under his influence, his god-children. Ernest Hello, the well-known lay theologian, and Georges Rouault, the renewer of religious painting in France, were likewise Bloy's friends and influenced by him. Among the enthusiastic admirers of Bloy were Albert Béguin, Daniel-Rops and Georges Bernanos. Bloy also made disciples outside France: Johannes Jörgensen, the Danish hagiographer and Nobel Prize winner, and Pieter van der Meer de Walcheren, the Dutch Catholic poet, became practising Catholics through Bloy. Giovanni Papini, Nikolai Berdyaev and Karl Pfleger acknowledge the importance of Bloy's criticism of his age. Ernst Jünger found the reading of Bloy "invigorating . . . and a real antidote to the age and its debilitating influence", and considers that his "real effect springs from the fact that he portrays man in his wickedness, but also in his glory." He calls Bloy "a tower rising from the marsh up to the heights" and predicts that his influence will increase: "Bloy is not yet a classic, but he will be one day."

SELECT BIBLIOGRAPHY

The works of all the English writers discussed in this book and translations of the best-known foreign ones are obtainable in many editions, including popular series like the Everyman Library. But in some cases English translations either do not exist or are out of print: this is true of many of the German writers, especially those of the baroque period. A full list of translations from German literature up to 1922 (the vast majority of them now out of print) will be found in

MORGAN, B. Q.: *A Bibliography of German Literature in English Translation*, University of Wisconsin Studies in Language and Literature, 16, Madison, Wis., Univ. of Wisconsin Press, 1922.

In this series:

SPEAIGHT, Robert: *The Christian Theatre.*

General

BRERETON, Geoffrey: *A Short History of French Literature*, Harmondsworth and Baltimore, Penguin Books, 1954.

COHEN, J. M.: *A History of Western Literature*, Harmondsworth and Baltimore, Penguin Books, 1956.

HUTTON, E.: *Catholicism and English Literature*, London, Muller, 1942.

O'DONNELL, D.: *Maria Cross*, London and New York, Oxford Univ. Press, 1953.

Sixteenth century

AUCLAIR, Marcelle: *Saint Teresa of Avila*, London, Burns & Oates, and New York, Pantheon, 1953.

BRODRICK, J., S.J.: *St Ignatius of Loyola: the Pilgrim Years*, London, Burns & Oates, and New York, Farrar Strauss, 1956.

BRUNO, F. DE J.-M., O.C.D.: *John of the Cross*, London, Sheed and Ward, and New York, Benziger, 1932.

CAMPBELL, W. E.: *More's Utopia and His Social Teaching*, London, Eyre and Spottiswoode, 1930; *Erasmus, Tyndale and More*, London, Eyre and Spottiswoode, 1949.

GRISAR, H.: *Martin Luther, His Life and Work*, Westminster, Md, Newman Press, 1950.

HOLLIS, Christopher: *Thomas More*, London, Burns & Oates, 1961 (Paperback edn), Milwaukee, Bruce, 1934.

IGNATIUS OF LOYOLA, St: *Spiritual Exercises* with a commentary by W. H. Longridge, London, Longmans, and New York, Morehouse, 1919: *Letters to Women*, translated by K. Pond and S. A. H. Weetman, London and New York, Herder-Nelson, 1960.

JOHN OF THE CROSS, St: *The Complete Works of St John of the Cross*, translated and edited by E. Allison Peers, three volumes, London, Burns & Oates, and Westminster, Md, Newman Press, 1953.

PEERS, E. Allison: *Handbook to the Life and Times of St Teresa and St John of the Cross*, London, Burns & Oates, and Westminster, Md, Newman Press, 1954; *St Teresa of Jesus and other Essays and Addresses*, London, Faber, and Philadelphia, Dufour, 1953; *Studies of the Spanish Mystics*, two volumes, London, S.P.C.K., and New York, Macmillan, 1927–30.

SACKVILLE-WEST, V. M.: *The Eagle and the Dove*, London, Michael Joseph and New York, Doubleday, 1944.

Seventeenth century

BEDOYÈRE, M. de la: *The Archbishop and the Lady: the story of Fénelon and Mme Guyon*, London, Collins, 1956.

BRERETON, Geoffrey: *Jean Racine, A Critical Biography*, London, Cassell, 1951.

BUNYAN, John: *Pilgrim's Progress*, ed. by J. B. Wharey, 2nd edition revised by Roger Sharrock, Oxford, Clarendon Press, 1960.

CRASHAW, Richard: *Poems, English, Latin and Greek*, ed. by L. C. Martin, London and New York, Oxford Univ. Press, 1927.

DONNE, John: *Poems*, two volumes, ed. by H. J. C. Grierson, London and New York, Oxford Univ. Press, 1912.

FORSTER, L. (Editor): *The Penguin Book of German Verse*, Harmondsworth and Baltimore, Penguin Books, 1957. (This anthology contains many poems, with prose translations, by the 17th- and 19th-century poets discussed in this book.

FRANCIS DE SALES, St: *Introduction to the Devout Life*, translated by Michael Day, London, Burns & Oates, and Westminster, Md, Newman Press, 1956; *Selected Letters*, translated with an Introduction by Elizabeth Stopp, London, Faber, 1960.

LANCASTER, H. C.: *A History of French Dramatic Literature*, 1610–1700, 9 vols., Baltimore, Johns Hopkins Press, 1929–42.

McCABE, W. H.: *An Introduction to the Early Jesuit Theatre*, Cambridge and New York, Cambridge Univ. Press, 1929.

MILTON, John: *Complete Works*, ed. F. A. Patterson, eighteen volumes, New York, Columbia Univ. Press, 1931–40.

PARKER, A. A.: *The Allegorical Drama of Calderon*, London, Dolphin, 1943.

PASCAL, Blaise: *Pensées* (French and English Text) trans. and edited by H. F. Stewart, London, Kegan Paul, and New York, Pantheon, 1950.

SANDERS, E. K.: *Bossuet, A Study*, London, S.P.C.K., 1921.

Nineteenth century

BOUYER, Louis: *Newman, His Life and Spirituality*, translated by J. L. May, London, Burns Oates, and New York, P. J. Kenedy, 1958.

CARLYLE, Thomas: *Critical and Miscellaneous Essays*, volume 2, New York, Page, 1949. (Essay on Novalis.)

D'HERBIGNY, M.: *Soloviev, a Russian Newman*, London, Burns & Oates, 1918.

DOSTOEVSKY, Fyodor: *Novels*, translated by Constance Garnett, twelve volumes, London and New York, Macmillan, 1912–20.

DUBOIS, E. T.: *Portrait of Léon Bloy*, London and New York, Sheed and Ward, 1950.

HOPKINS, Gerard Manley: *Notebooks and Papers*, edited by Humphrey House, London and New York, Oxford Univ. Press, 1937; *Poems*, edited by Robert Bridges and W. H. Gardner, London and New York, Oxford Univ. Press, 1948.

KIERKEGAARD, Søren: *Complete Works*, translated by W. Lowrie and others, London and New York, Oxford Univ. Press, 1938– (twenty volumes have appeared to date).

NEWMAN, John Henry, Cardinal: *A Newman Synthesis*, arranged by Erich Przywara, London and New York, Sheed and Ward, 1930; *Prose and Poetry* selected by Geoffrey Tillotson, London, Hart-Davis and Cambridge, Mass., Harvard Univ. Press, 1957.

POLIMENI, Emanuela: *Léon Bloy, the Pauper Prophet*, New York Philosophical Library, 1951.

THOMPSON, Francis: *Poems*, London, Hollis and Carter, 1946; *Complete Poems*, New York, Modern Library, 1947.